K20-61

The Pleasure of Poetry With and By Children:

a handbook

by

VARDINE MOORE

The Scarecrow Press, Inc.
Metuchen, N.J. & London
1981

Poems by Melinda Moore (pages 4-5) were originally published in The Horn Book Magazine. Reprinted by permission of the publisher.
Poems by the children listed on page 8 originally appeared
in the broadsides Writing Regulars and The Writing Basket,
printed by The Evansville Public Library and Vanderburgh
Public Library, Evansville, Indiana. Used by permission.
Poem by Joshua MacKenzie (page 4) was originally published
in The Christian Science Monitor (May 3, 1976). Reprinted
by permission from The Christian Science Monitor, © 1976
The Christian Science Publishing Society. All rights re-
served.

Library of Congress Cataloging in Publication Data

Moore, Vardine, 1906-
    The pleasure of poetry with and by children.

    Bibliography: p.
    Includes index.
    1. Poetry and children.   I. Title.
PN1085.M63   808.06'81   80-29015
ISBN 0-8108-1399-8

Dedicated
with love and gratitude
to all the librarians and all the children
whose inspiration and co-operation
prove constant.

CONTENTS

ACKNOWLEDGMENTS

So many have helped me realize this book that it is not possible to mention each one by name: to all of you I extend my sincere thanks.

My gratitude is extended to Miss Bernice Bruner who, as head of the Division of Work with Schools and Children in the Evansville and Vanderburgh County Public Libraries, first suggested offering a creative writing club for children in the library.

I am also grateful to Peggy Jack, Director of the Institute for the Fine and Performing Arts at the University of Evansville, for the opportunity of teaching creative poetry in the summer program for children.

My thanks go to Robert W. Mitchner, former Director of the Indiana University Writers' Conference, for inviting me to be on his staff, and to the leaders of poetry workshops I attended there who increased my love and understanding of poetry: Rolfe Humphries, Lionel Wiggam, Winfield Townley Scott, John Ashbery, William Jay Smith, Gwendolyn Brooks, Arthur Gregor, Sandra Hockman, and David Wagoner, along with poets whose children's literature workshops I attended: Charlotte Zolotow, Beatrice de Regniers, and Madeleine L'Engle.

My appreciation goes to Marianna Joest and Judy Meadows for help with typing and organization; to Eugene Gula, grade teacher, for proofreading and arrangement; to Robert McDowell, Poet-in-Residence at Indiana State University--Evansville, for critical reading of the manuscript; and to Marianna Tredway and Marilyn Kluger for advice and encouragement.

I wish to express my thanks for the children's poems which appear in this book by the following young contributors:

Mark Alcott
Danny Baker
William Barnett
Amy Baum
Amy Biggs
Angela Brown
Graeme Browning
Trip Browning
Lillian Faye Cabage
Ann Carpenter
James Clardy
Kenneth Clardy
Shelly Cook
Leann Cox
Jean Coyle
Fred Creech
John Danner
Teri Darrington
Nan Diekmann
Joe Elliott
Emily Everett
Jackie Ewing
Kim Ewing
Pam Ewing
Robert Fleming
Kristin Forbes
Tim Freson
Ann Georgesen
Philip Goodloe
Thomas Goodloe
Kimberly Grigsby
Heather Himebaugh
Mary Hughes
Carolyn Johnson
Frank Kanowsky
Bruce Kell
Melanie Kell
Lee Kellems
Scott Kirves
Andrea Klinger
Lisa Klinger
Bob Kluger
Stefi Lepko
Sara E. Lesch
Ruth Linstromberg

Sarah McCray
Patricia McElroy
Joshua Mackenzie
Susan McKinney
Patrick McMillan
Tonya Madison
Barbara Martin
Cheryl Martin
Kathy Martin
Tatiana Matysuk
Elizabeth Miley
John Lee Monyhan
Melinda Moore
Mary Louise Moutoux
Gail Mulholland
Autumn Newsome
David Pannkuk
Kenneth Pferrer
Rebecca Pfettscher
Kari Points
Elijah Pritchett
Nancy Purtzer
Vickie Purtzer
Jeanne Roller
Kristin Rusche
Susie Rusche
Laurie Schlueter
Mark Seib
Lori Seiler
Colleen Sharer
Judy Shepard
Shara Sights
Susan Small
Karen Smith
Karl Sowa
Carolyn Sparks
Diana Stevens
Suzanne Suhrheinrich
Marco Talbert
Maria Talbert
Lynn Trockman
Becky Underwood
Shawn Williams
John Wittenbraker
Jennie Woodworth

PREFACE

Many years ago I became aware that poetry is the natural language of young children. The essence of poetry is heard in their rhythmic, imaginative, original and sometimes nonsensical speech. I began to collect these delightful sayings of all children I was privileged to be near.

As a teacher in nursery school and later in preschool story hour at the Evansville (Ind.) Public Libraries, my collection and my interest grew. Miss Bernice Bruner, then head of the Division of Work with Schools and Children, asked if I would lead a creative writing group for older children. I was glad for the opportunity to encourage the gift of creative language which is inherent in young children before school age.

Teachers, librarians and parents respond enthusiastically to workshops in which we share experiences in recognizing and nurturing the creative spark. I have found that going into the classrooms of kindergarten through eighth grade by invitation of the Arts and Education Council of Evansville to participate in the program of Artists in the Schools is productive and gratifying. It is also an inspiration for me to teach creative poetry at the University of Evansville in the summer program for children offered by the Institute of the Fine and Performing Arts.

Using poetry with children is an ongoing surprise and as delightful as poetry itself has been described.

Vardine Moore
Evansville, Indiana
September 1980

ix

Chapter 1

COO ME A POEM, BABY

All children seem to be born poets. A baby cooing and babbling in the crib is trying out a natural, satisfying approach to language. These spontaneous sounds have many of the basic elements of poetry with rhythm and cadence recognizable in their first delightful adventures in communication.

Scientific studies prove that during the first months of life, babies vocalize by cooing, gurgling, sputtering, fussing and crying. Although there are no intelligible words, there is definite meaning in all this varied polyphony: "I'm comfortable," "I'm happy," "I'm angry," "I'm in pain."

Babbling usually begins between two months and six months of age and consists of vowel and consonant combinations, such as ma-ma, da-da, goo-goo, ba-ba, repeated over and over with obvious enjoyment. Again, further qualities of poetry can be detected. Added to the rhythm of the babbling (often accompanied by rhythmic movements of arms and legs or of the entire body) rhyme, repetition, and alliteration appear. Perhaps the baby is cooing a poem and does not yet have the accepted vocabulary to translate some magical communication.

The eighteenth-century poet William Wordsworth may have understood this when he wrote in "Intimations of Immortality,"

> ... trailing clouds of glory do we come
> From God, who is our home:
> Heaven lies about us in our infancy:

1

Wordsworth's contemporary, the poet William Blake, must also have believed that babies have a divine spark of creativity which we cannot immediately fathom, and he expressed this belief in "Songs of Innocence":

"I have no name;
I am but two days old. "
What shall I call thee?
"I happy am.
Joy is my name. "
Sweet joy befall thee!

When babies are about a year old, these random syllables begin to form single words: milk, shoe, hot, my, dog (although for a while this last word may keep the rhyming, onomatopoeic "bow-wow"). Two-word combinations often continue to rhyme because children find the sound pleasing, and it is easier to say "night-night" than "good-night" and "bye-bye" than "good-bye. " The use of one word utterances is followed rapidly by sentence fragments: "Milk hot, " "my shoe. " The advancement of language skills expands until normal children by the age of five or six have a vocabulary of approximately 2500 words and are capable of handling sentence patterns with ease.

Researchers in language development report that the first babbling sounds are common to almost all languages and that babies around the world produce the same vowels and consonants. Then, at about six months of age it is possible to distinguish the native tongue, whether the babbling is English, Russian, German or some other language, according to speech heard during this time.

In vocal communication, children learn vocabulary very quickly in the early years from hearing adults talk to them long before the words they hear have any meaning. The fortunate ones hear lullabies and nursery rhymes from the beginning. The baby listens with rapt attention to "This little pig went to market, this little pig stayed home. This little pig had roast beef, and this little pig had none, and this little pig went crying 'wee-wee-wee-wee' all the way home. " There is enchantment in these words long before knowledge of markets or roast beef. Not only are the rhythm and rhyme pleasing to the ear, but the physical contact of counting and wiggling each little pink toe adds warmth and delight to the language experience.

The development of writing and of art forms has been

observed to follow a similar spiral of growth as language development. At about the age of two, children begin to scrib-
ble in random scratches, seemingly senseless to the adult eye.
However, it has been discovered that there are twenty or so
basic scribbles made by children at a very young age, which
follow definite, recognizable direction; all sorts of lines--ver-
tical, horizontal, diagonal, circular, curving, and waving with
emphatic dots--appear frequently. Movements of the hand and
arm seem to bring a satisfying feeling to the scribbler. A
blank space contains something that did not exist before--a
truly creative experience unfolds.

Later, intentional shapes can be detected; circles and
squares, crosses within each, lines radiating from circles,
and many designs found in prehistoric caves, carved on stone
in jungles and on primitive pottery. This artistic impulse is
universal; children in every country all over the world follow
the same progress in the same way at approximately the same
age. The sun is depicted as a circle with lines radiating
from the perimeter, human figures are stick-like with round
heads and stick-like arms, often extending from the head.
Trees are straight lines with branches shooting from the top.
A scientific study of this subject is treated in great depth by
Rhoda Kellogg with Scott O'Dell in The Psychology of Children's Art.

With beginnings of poetry as with the beginnings of
art, the wise adult will not insist upon conformity or more
sophisticated forms of expression. Children grow and develop
from good examples and from encouragement and appreciation of
their beginning efforts. The touch of hands along with the whole
chanting of "Pat-a-cake, pat-a-cake, baker's man" or "Pease
porridge hot" evokes a sunny smile and a hushed air of ex-
pectancy. Lullabies supply the beauty and magic of words
as well as gentle, soothing melodies to the child cradled in
loving arms.

Poetry and syllables arranged in rhythmic cadence are
important and delightful means for stimulating a child's interest in words and language growth. Poetry should be offered
in the same tone of voice and manner as ordinary speech,
not recited in a lofty or sing-songy way.

From the earliest stages of life, poetry should be
part of every child's nourishment, a rightful heritage, whether
chanted, sung, or read aloud. It follows naturally that children frequently sing or chant their own word patterns in return on the spur of the moment. For these young singers

do not deliberately set out to compose poetry, particularly
a poem to order or on command. The words simply express
an awareness, or stream forth, triggered by excitement or
emotion in poetic form and language.

In his book, A Journey of Discovery, Ian Southall ob-
serves, "Children often crystallize moments of intense emotion
into poems of rare beauty." One summer day my next door
neighbor Ann, at age three, called me to the back door and,
very excited, gave me a little jewel:

> Come and see the tents we made.
> We made them on the lines;
> Not the lines in the zoo,
> Nor the lines that eat you up,
> But the lines you hang clothes on.

Sara, almost three, becoming aware of birth and
life, told her grandmother an inmost thought in a rhymed
couplet:

> Before I was born I was a piece of the air,
> And I followed you around everywhere.

A friend told me that one windy morning at the breakfast table, her son Joshua, at age four, began to sway rhyth-
mically in his chair, chanting with gusto:

> Oh how the wind blows!
> Oh how the crane swings
> And the ocean waves.
> Oh how good!
> Oh how the crane swings,
> Swings bricks and wood.
> Oh how good!
>   --Joshua MacKenzie

I was first aware of this poetic approach to language
when my own daughter Melinda at an early age sometimes
shared with me deeply-felt observations. I quickly jotted
down the words, exactly as they came, on the back of an
envelope or handy scrap of paper, or added them to a gro-
cery list to be transferred later to a notebook, just as
parents record "Baby's First Words" in a Baby Book. It
is equally important to record combinations of words as
ability to handle language increases.

After walking around the massive trunk of a hundred-

year-old tree in our front yard, Melinda came inside quietly
and spoke these lines:

> God is our world
> All in peace.
> He stands still like a tree.
> He doesn't run all around the yard
> And make people nervous.

Her story-poem crystallized in a more whimsical vein:

> There is a little fairy
> Called Me.
> Deep in the woods I live
> With witches and rabbits and squirrels.
>
> I am a very tiny creature,
> So if you do not like me,
> Please do not harm me.

A little boy who was visiting in our home with his
parents at that time was so taken with the last stanza, that
he quickly memorized and quoted it to his parents at appropriate times of crisis in the family.

With Melinda, as it had with Joshua, a windy day
stirred up an emotional response with lilting rhythm:

> Blow, blow, blow,
> Wind in the skies.
> Blow the rain through the trees.
> Bend the trees,
> Bend the limbs.
> Bend everything.
>
> It's good for the vegetables,
> The squash, tomatoes, and corn.
> It's good for little children
> To go puddling in.

Inadvertent rhyme often shows up as it does in this poem
of emotional content:

> When it storms in the night,
> When it glooms in the night,
> And the dark is full of fear,
> Your step is the rushing

> Of angel wings.
> I want you near.

Pre-schoolers, whether at home, in library story
hours, nursery school or other group situations, frequently
express an emotion or exciting experience in poetic form
with rhythm, rhyme, alliteration, repetition and imagery.
A poem may come at any time. It's fun to recognize poetry
which comes spontaneously from children and to jot it down
before it slips into oblivion.

Judy, in nursery school, shouted at another child,
red-faced in anger:

> Bottle-baby,
> Bottle-baby,
> Suck a nipple, suck a nipple.
> Suck, suck, suck!

In contrast, Ellen, in a voice full of love and tender humor,
announced one day:

> We got Tigger at home with blue eyes,
> A little white kitty with blue eyes,
> Sometimes he bites my toes.

This is a good example of a triplet form with the musical
devices of slant end rhyme and counterpoint in the first
two lines.

At a pre-school story hour in the library, Tonya
relived a vivid experience in a patterned poem with dramatic
cadence:

> The moon was over our garage,
> I saw it peeping down at me.
> Then we went for a ride
> And the moon followed our car.
> After a while it began to rain
> And the rain washed the moon away.

Kathy was inspired to tell her little story sung in
mournful tones with face to match:

> Come home, little doggie, come home.
> We love you, little doggie,
> Come home.

> Come home, little horsie, come home.
> We love you, little horsie,
> Come home.

This went on verse after verse, imploring every animal she could think of to come home, until it was time for the children themselves to go home.

Children are very adept at making comparisons and word pictures in creative language:

> "When I look at the sun, my eyes get out of breath."

> "Mothers look so pretty; just like a pink color crayon."

> "That noise sounds like splinters."

> "An escalator looks like a stairway.
> You ride to the top,
> Then off you hop."

When I asked a little boy, "When will you come to see me again?" he replied, "When the leaves come down and the snow falls."

Anyone hearing such melodic and imaginative speech must agree with the Russian author Kornei Chukovsky when he says, in From Two to Five, "Enchanting children's speech! It will never cease to give me joy." His observations and examples show how children approach mastery of their native tongue whether in Russian or English. In his first chapter, "A Linguistic Genius," he records the following "overheards":

> [A little girl muttering in her sleep]: "Mom, cover my hind leg."

> "Daddy, look how your pants are sulking!"

> "Oh Mommy, how balloony your legs are!"

> (Or a bit of dialogue): "My daddy himself told me that...." "My mommie herself told me that...."
> "But my daddy is himselfer than your mommie—my daddy is much more himselfer...."

Chukovsky finds pleasure in children's observations that a
bald man had a barefoot head ... that a mint candy made a
draft in the mouth, that the husband of a grasshopper was
a daddyhopper. It appears that children use words and interpret them in original expression in every language.

Sparks of imagination catch fire at varying age levels,
kindled by sense experiences through eyes, ears, nose, skin
and muscles in a widening world of contacts. Increased
awareness of the outside world gives color and flavor to
expression when fused with the child's magic inner world.
Thomas Edison, when asked the secret of his inventive
genius, replied, "I listen from within." While listening
from within, the child's imagination expands by exploring
the unknown and by seeing the world with fresh eyes. Imagination, in the words of Shakespeare, "Gives to airy no-
things local habitation and a name."

As adults we can contribute to this on-going miracle
of linguistic skill by recognition, appreciation and nourishment, not by over-zealous praise nor with an eye to pre-
mature publication. Using poetry with and by children has
rewards far outreaching aggrandizement.

The human spirit, from infancy on, needs communi-
cation--someone to listen. The inter-play of creative language helps a child to discover himself and the world around
him. It extends imagination, vocabulary, and interest in
the music of words.

Poetry and rhythmic speech are among the most
delightful tools for developing a child's mastery of native
speech and provide an incentive for learning to read.

Robert Frost once said that life needs "toning up,"
and that poetry is one of the best means of toning things
up. All of these goals can be accomplished through an
awareness of the qualities of poetry, a listening ear, and a
loving, caring heart.

Chapter 2

"BUT I HATE POETRY"

A negative response to the word "poetry" is sometimes expressed by children and by adults who have lost their trails of glory for one reason or another. Usually they have forgotten what poetry is. Ask poetry-haters, "What is poetry?" and you are likely to get a variety of answers:

> "It's poetry if it's hard to understand."

> "It's poetry if it uses dumb words like o'er and doth and would'st, or if it uses words too big and fancy."

> "It's poetry if it rhymes," or, "I hate it because it doesn't rhyme."

> "It's poetry if it's sing-songy."

No wonder they hate "poetry." However, there are many definitions of poetry; none are final, and none are acceptable to everybody. So you may take your choice or make up one of your own.

What Is Poetry?

One dictionary neatly sidesteps the question by this definition: "Poetry is the material out of which poems are made." Another goes a bit further: "Poetry is an arrange-

ment of words in lines, usually with a regularly repeated
accent and often with rhyme." An encyclopedia states:
"Absolute poetry is the concrete and artistic expression of
the human mind in emotional and rhythmical language."

Carl Sandburg considered thirty-eight definitions as
his own personal choice. Some of these are:

Poetry is a pack-sack of invisible keepsakes.

Poetry is the achievement of the synthesis of
hyacinths and biscuits.

Poetry is the capture of a picture, a song, or a
flair, in a deliberate prism of words.

Gwendolyn Brooks says she has but one definition: "Poetry
is life distilled." The poet Rolfe Humphries gave the members of our creative poetry workshop at Indiana University
his definition: "Poetry is technically human speech made
musical by art and vitally intense communication of meaning."

To present poetry to children effectively, you as the
teacher must be familiar with basic techniques. This is
necessary for your own awareness and to help children understand the elements of poetry as they grow from appreciation
to participation in the creative process of writing poetry.

The Word

The first element is, of course, the word. As we
have mentioned, children love the sounds of words and word-
play from the beginning, even before they know their meanings. It is fascinating to discover the mystery of language
by putting words together.

Single words have personalities of their own; some
harsh, some soft. They can be musical or they can be dull.
Words can make pictures in the mind. These words create
an image by appealing to the five senses of seeing, hearing,
touching, tasting and smelling. Lack-luster words such as
"just," "very," "so," "quite" sometimes creep in as fillers,
often used to keep a regular beat which the writer mistakenly
thinks is demanded. Other words that interfere with the
intense communication of meaning are those known as clichés.
A cliché is a word or phrase that has lost its original power

and freshness because it has been overused and because it
is obvious. "Blue as the sky," "cold as ice," "green as
grass" are tired, worn-out expressions. The best words
arranged in the best order will be found in the best poetry.

Rhythm

        Perhaps the second most distinctive element in poetry
is rhythm. Children delight in rhythm and rhyme, but even-
tually find rhythm more important than rhyme. A. A.
Milne, who recognized this in his intriguing original rhythms,
has said that every piece of poetry has a music of its own
which is humming to itself as it goes along, and every line,
every word in it has to keep time to the music, which may
be jolly or melancholy, marching, dancing, galloping or
plodding.

        Rhythm is a natural part of life, the closest rhythm
being the regular beat of the heart. Night follows day; one
season follows another in regular sequence. The rings inside a tree trunk, leaves placed along a stem have a rhythmic
pattern or design. Nature is rhythmic rather than chaotic,
and so is the best poetry.

        However, rhythm in poetry should not be as relentless
as the beat of a metronome. Even strictly metered verse
has some metrical variety to avoid monotony. The meter
of much modern poetry is loosened to flow down the page
like a waterfall. Modern poets for some time have written
free verse, which uses cadence rather than meter. Irregular
rhythms are not new. The poetry of the Bible has cadence
but not meter. When cadenced verse is read aloud, the
voice rises and falls in little waves.

        Beautiful use of cadence is found in The Song of
Solomon (chapter two, verses eleven and twelve):

            For, lo, the winter is past,
            the rain is over and gone;
            the flowers appear on the earth;
            the time of the singing of birds is come,
            and the voice of the turtle is heard in our land.

        Regular rhythm is achieved by the use of metrics
rather than cadence. Metrical verse consists of stressed
and unstressed syllables in lines of various lengths. Each

stressed syllable is called a foot or beat. The most familiar
are shown on the following chart.

NAME	MARK	EXAMPLES	BEAT
iamb (iambic) The most commonly used poetic foot	- /	- / surprise - / the boy - / forgive	ta-TUM
trochee (trochaic) Also commonly used	/ -	/ - pretty / - softly / - / - Hiawatha	TUM-ta
anapest (anapestic) Most commonly used with iambic and trochaic for variety	- - /	- - / understand - - / it is here - - / spread your wings	ta-ta-TUM
dactyl (dactylic) A swinging rhythm, seldom found throughout a poem	/ - -	/ - - everywhere / - - natural / - - navigate	TUM-ta-ta
spondee Used for emphasis and variety	/ /	/ / bright star / / get out	TUM-TUM

As you will notice in the following examples, the entire verse is made up principally of one kind of foot, with another kind thrown in occasionally. Otherwise, it could sound very monotonous. This is true of most good poetry. Iambus is a two-syllable foot with stress or accent on the second syllable:

> Jack Sprat could eat no fat,
> His wife could eat no lean;
> And so, betwixt them both,
> They ate the platter clean.
>
> --Mother Goose

Trochee is a two-syllable foot with accent on the first syllable:

> Peter, Peter, pumpkin eater
> Had a wife and couldn't keep her;
>
> --Mother Goose

Anapest is a three-syllable foot with accent on the third syllable:

> Old King Cole was a merry old soul,
>   And a merry old soul was he.
> He called for his pipe and he called for his bowl,
>   And he called for his fiddlers three.
>
> --Mother Goose

Dactyl is a three-syllable foot with accent on the first syllable:

> "Pussycat, pussycat
>   Where have you been?"
> "I've been to London
>   To look at the Queen."
> "Pussycat, pussycat,
>   What did you there?"
> "I frightened a little mouse
>   Under her chair."
>
> --Mother Goose

Spondee is a two-syllable foot with stress on both syllables. The first line of many Mother Goose rhymes uses the spondee:

> Fee, Fi, Fo, Fum
>
> Baa, baa, black sheep

Poems have lines of different lengths and are named according to the number of accented syllables or feet in the line. A one-foot line is called a <u>monometer</u>. Few poems are written entirely in monometer, but this type of line is often used as a refrain in poems of other meters. The following example illustrates the use of monometer in refrain:

> The north wind doth blow,
>   We soon shall have snow,
> And what will poor Robin do then?
>   Poor thing!
>
> He'll sit in a barn,
> To keep himself warm,
> And hide his head under his wing.
>   Poor thing!
>
> --Mother Goose

This old counting-out rhyme uses monometer throughout:

> Onery,
> Twoery,
> Ickery,
> Ann,
> Philison,
> Pholison,
> Nicholas,
> Jan,
> Queevy,
> Quavy,
> English navy,
> Stinklum,
> Stanklum,
> Buck!

A two-foot line is called a <u>dimeter</u>:

> "To bed, to bed!"
> Said Sleepyhead.

A three-foot line is called a <u>trimeter</u>:

> One misty, moisty morning.

A four-foot line is called a <u>tetrameter</u>:

> Humpty Dumpty sat on a wall.

A five-foot line is called a pentameter:

> Christmas is coming, the geese are getting fat.

A six-foot line is called a hexameter:

> I had a little husband no bigger than my thumb.

A seven-foot line is called a heptameter:

> Simple Simon met a pieman going to the fair.

An eight-foot line is called an octometer. The first and third lines in each stanza of Edgar Allan Poe's "Raven" are good examples of octometer:

Once upon a midnight dreary, while I pondered weak and weary,

The number of feet in a line of English verse rarely exceeds eight, but it is possible for verses to contain more. Ordinarily a poet would not begin by choosing a particular meter except, perhaps, as an experiment or for fun. A poem usually begins with a single line singing itself over and over in the poet's mind with its own stressed and unstressed syllables, which continue with some regularity throughout the poem.

Rhyme

Exact rhyme is an easily recognized element of poetry and is often considered by beginners as an essential, which is a mistaken idea as Eve Merriam points out in two of her delightful books of poetry for children, It Doesn't Have to Rhyme and There Is No Rhyme for Silver.

In rhymed poems, we discover a variety of patterns which can be designated by letters of the alphabet and traced throughout the poem. Thus a will rhyme with a, b, with b, c, with c, and so on, wherever the rhyming word falls.

Hey, diddle diddle!	(a)
The cat and the fiddle	(a)
The cow jumped over the moon;	(b)
The little dog laughed to see such sport	(c)
And the dish ran away with the spoon.	(b)

-- Mother Goose

Handy Pandy, Jack-a-dandy,   (a)
Loves plum cake and sugar candy.   (a)
He bought some at a grocer's shop,   (b)
And out he came, hop, hop, hop.   (b)
                                    --Mother Goose

Little Miss Muffet   (a)
Sat on a tuffet,   (a)
Eating of curds and whey.   (b)
There came a big spider   (c)
And sat down beside her   (c)
And frightened Miss Muffet away.   (b)
                                    --Mother Goose

The Lion and the Unicorn were fighting for the
crown,   (a)
The Lion beat the Unicorn all around the town, (a)
Some gave them white bread, and some gave them
brown,   (a)
Some gave them plum-cake, and sent them out
of town.   (a)
                                    --Mother Goose

Words usually rhyme at the end of a line, but we
find poetry that is constructed around other rhyme schemes.
Scattered rhyme or random rhyme is found in a poem with
rhyming words scattered throughout the poem in the same
way a painter balances a red here against a red there, or
as a musician plays a variation on a theme. This is like
telling a friend to drop in any time.

While a poem does not have to rhyme, the poet William Matthews tells his classes that there are so few vowels
in the English language, it is almost impossible not to rhyme.
It occasionally happens that someone will make a rhyme in-
advertently in ordinary conversation and hurriedly add, "I'm
a poet and don't know it."

An excellent example of internal rhyming is from
Edgar Allan Poe's "The Raven":

Once upon a midnight dreary, while I pondered weak and weary,
    Over many a quaint and curious volume of forgotten lore,
While I nodded, nearly napping, suddenly there came a tapping
    As of someone gently rapping, rapping at my chamber door ...

Beginners are particularly fond of rhyme. In her

class at The Indiana Writers' Conference, Frances Gray Patton, author of <u>Good Morning, Miss Dove</u>, related the conditions of a poem she composed at age three: "I was walking with my father past a lawn full of magnolia trees in which some remarkably unmusical birds, English sparrows, starlings, or maybe grackles, were making an unholy row." Mrs. Patton's spontaneous poem shows the ingenuity of young children in using rhyme:

> "The winds is blowing sawfly,
> The birds are singing awf'ly. "*

Exact rhyme is rather like an echo with repetition of the same vowel and consonant sounds. There are many other rhyming sounds. <u>Assonance rhyme</u> is characterized by identical vowel sounds with different consonant endings. Examples from Mother Goose:

"Little Tommy Tittlemouse"; fishes/ditches

"The North Wind Doth Blow"; barn/warm

"Little Tommy Tucker"; supper/butter

"The Girl and the Birds"; stone/home

<u>Consonant rhyming</u> is characterized by identical final consonant sounds with vowel sounds related: weak/pick, blood/mood. These combinations are called off-rhymes or slant rhymes. Mother Goose rhymes abound in consonant rhyme:

"Winter"; early/fairly

"Goosey, Goosey Gander"; wander/chamber

"Little Jenny Wren"; feet/bit

"The Seasons"; poppy/nippy

"Pippin Hill"; dirty/curtsy

"The Piper and His Cow"; penny/bonny

<u>Alliteration</u> is considered a rhyming device since the first

---

*Used by permission of the author.

letter of each word is repeated, giving a musical effect.
Lines from Mother Goose illustrate this pleasing result:

> Goosey, goosey gander....

> Pease porridge in the pot ...

> Wee Willie Winkie runs through the town ...

> Around the green gravel the grass grows green ...

> Diddle, diddle, dumpling, my son John ...

> This is the cock that crowed in the morn,
> That waked the priest all shaven and shorn,
> That married the man all tattered and torn.

A familiar Mother Goose rhyme uses alliteration
throughout the entire verse:

> Peter Piper picked a peck of pickled peppers;
> A peck of pickled peppers Peter Piper picked.
> If Peter Piper picked a peck of pickled peppers,
> Where's the peck of pickled peppers Peter Piper
> picked?

When alliteration is used so consistently, the verse
becomes a tongue-twister, which children enjoy trying to
emulate:

> Bob Birkley bought two blue birds in Benny's bird
> bungalow.
>
> > --Susan Small

> Little Lulu loves to live in the lilac tree over Larkin's
> Lane.
>
> > --John Danner

Much of Mother Goose relies upon Repetition for
rhyming effect:

> Hot Cross Buns!
>   Hot Cross Buns!
> One a penny, two a penny,
>   Hot Cross Buns!

> Needles and pins, needles and pins,
>   When a man marries, his trouble begins.

Repetition of words and phrases can be in any form the poet's inner ear dictates, as in these lines from "The Bells" by Edgar Allan Poe:

> Keeping time, time, time,
> In a sort of Runic rhyme,
>   To the throbbing of the bells,
>   Of the bells, bells, bells,
> To the sobbing of the bells.

The use of Refrain also gives a pleasing musical effect, which we find frequently in Mother Goose:

> Clap, clap handies,
>   Mammie's wee, wee ain;
> Clap, clap handies,
>   Daddie's comin' hame.
> Hame till his bonny wee bit laddie;
>   Clap, clap handies,
>   My wee, wee ain.

Experience with writing the haiku form helps children accept the fact that some very good poems disdain rhyme. The child feels free to express a thought just as it comes to him. Another book I like to use for examples of poems that do not rhyme is The Dog Writes on the Window with His Nose, a collection by David Kherdian with charming pictures by Nonny Hogrogian. A love of a book!

Form

When seen in print, poetry can usually be distinguished from prose by its form or pattern. The writer follows a certain structure, one which may adhere to a traditional style or be an experimental form. In either case, a poem has structure.

Children can be introduced to stanza form by poems selected for appreciation. These should be basic patterns found in most poems for children. Later they will discover more complicated forms. The simplest conventional forms are easily recognized even by beginners:

Couplet: a two line poem
Triplet: a three line poem
Quatrain: a four line poem
Cinquain: a five line poem

These forms make up different kinds of poetry, alone and in combination.

A couplet is easy to remember.   "A couple" of lines that may rhyme at the end or may not.

Rhymed:

Acorn, acorn at my feet,
Acorn, acorn, sits in a seat.
                    --Kim Ewing

Unrhymed:

Snow in the moonlight
Is silver and blue.
                    --Pam Ewing

Children have a lot of fun thinking up couplets of two or more words that rhyme. One that they might see every day on the way to school is this sign:

GO
SLOW

This form, sometimes called terse verse, is made more humorous and interesting by giving it a long title.

WHAT MOTHER SAID TO MY CAT
WHEN SHE TURNED OVER A
VASE OF FLOWERS.

"Scat,
Cat."

A TRICK I TAUGHT MY DOG.

"Roll over,
Rover."

Making up terse verse continues outside of class. Karl Sowa, who was in the university poetry class and also in the mime class, slipped down the aisle during intermission at a concert and whispered to me,

"After mime time,
Comes rhyme time."

Children easily understand the word <u>triplet</u>, a three-line poem which may have a variety of rhyme schemes or none at all.

LATE SNOW

Snow on the leaves
And a little breeze
Form a silver Spring.
        --Kim Ewing

WIND

Have you ever listened to the wind blow?
It rocks the trees
And blows the leaves.
        --Diana Stevens

RAIN

It sounds like the tap of a shoemaker's hammer
It feels like the touch of a fairy.
Spring rain.
        --John Lee Monyhan

Another three-line poem popular with children is the ancient Japanese form called haiku. Instead of meter and rhyme, it consists of seventeen syllables. The first line contains five syllables, the second line seven syllables, and the last line five again.

These translations from the ancient poets of haiku are easily understood by children of today.

Get out of my way
And allow me to plant these
Bamboos, Mr. Toad.
        --Miura Chora

On the shining roof
the boy's abandoned string ball
Soaking up spring rain.
        --Buson

Children are eager to try the haiku form.

The willow whistle

I carry to school each day
Is very dried up.
                    --Patricia McElroy

Little Fir Tree small
Covered over by snow drifts.
Come sit by my fire.
                    --Carolyn Johnson

   The four line quatrain is the most familiar form to
children since most nursery rhymes and traditional verse
are written in this form.

Humpty Dumpty sat on a wall,
   Humpty Dumpty had a great fall;
All the King's horses and all the King's men
   Couldn't put Humpty Dumpty together again.
                    --Mother Goose

AN ATOM

An atom is smaller than small;
It is smaller than any ball.
It is so small
You can't see it at all.
                    --John Wittenbraker

SPRING

Golden days and cloud-filled skies
Pretty dancing butterflies.
The robin with its bright red vest.
I think I like spring days the best.
                    --Susan McKinney

   A poem of five lines is called a cinquain. It may be
of any rhyme scheme and of any meter, with any line length,
or it may be free verse.   A syllable cinquain is fun to try.
The first line has two syllables, the second line has four
syllables, the third line has six, the fourth has eight, and
the fifth line goes back to two syllables.

Potter,
Mugs, cups, bowls, plates.
They are made out of clay.
At first messy, then dry, then fired.
Artist.
                    --Elizabeth Miley

> Kittens,
> Furry and soft,
> Fighting, playing, mewing.
> I really like baby kittens.
> Kindle.
>
> --David Pannkuk

Adelaide Crapsey developed a formal, unrhymed poem pattern in five lines containing consecutive lines of 1, 2, 3, 4, and 1 foot, all iambic. This specific form is called a cinquain, although the term is used for any five-line stanza.

An interesting five-line poem which encourages children to try some of their own is the tanka, which is related to the haiku and also popular in Japan. The tanka, a thirty-one syllable poem, follows the pattern of 5-7-5-7-7 syllables if strictly composed. After trying the tanka form, children are encouraged to write poems of five lines without any specific number of syllables.

STARS

> The stars are like nymphs dancing,
> The Moon is their Queen,
> The sky is their ballroom.
> Until the sun comes up
> And scares them all away.
>
> --Melanie Kell

> Raking the newly cut grass,
> I hate that.
> The cut grass covers
> The growing grass
> Like a blanket.
>
> --Kim Ewing

There are many formalized five-line poems with classic names, which can come later in the study of poetry, but it should be pointed out that a five-line poem can be composed of a quatrain and a single line, usually a refrain. It can also be a combination of a triplet and a couplet. There are many free forms of a five-line poem.

The most familiar five-line poem is a limerick, appreciated by all ages. The five lines use strict meter and rhyme scheme. The meter is essentially anapestic with three stresses in the first, second and fifth lines and with two stresses in the third and fourth. In form, a rhyming

couplet of three stresses is followed by another rhyming
couplet of two stresses, ending with a three-stress line
rhyming with the first couplet. After hearing many limericks,
children catch the rhythm in a short time. The most famous
limericks are those of Edward Lear.

> There was a young Lady whose bonnet
> Came untied when the birds sat upon it;
>   But she said, "I don't care!
>   All the birds in the air
> Are welcome to sit on my bonnet!"
>   --Lear

> There was an old man on a hill,
> Who seldom, if ever, stood still;
>   He ran up and down
>   In his grandmother's gown,
> Which adorned that old man on a hill.
>   --Lear

> There was an Old Man with a nose,
> Who said, "If you choose to suppose
>   That my nose is too long,
>   You are certainly wrong!"
> That remarkable man with a nose.
>   --Lear

Even the youngest like to try writing a limerick and often
come up with some as good as the classics by the famous
Mr. Lear.

> There was a young girl named Ann
> Who ate all her food from one pan.
>   "Dishwashing I hate,
>   So I won't use a plate.
> I'll eat all my food from one pan."
>   --Melanie Kell

> There was a young man from France,
> Who wanted to learn how to dance,
>   He said, "Dancing is fun,
>   But I'm not the one.
> All I can do is prance."
>   --Gail Mulholland

> There once was a boy named Dennis
> Who simply loved to play tennis

> When he hit the ball
> It was lost until Fall
> And that is what happened to Dennis
> > --Marco Talbert

Vital Communication

After seeing how poetry "is technically human speech made musical by art," the next step is to discover how poetry is made "vital by intense communication of meaning." It comes about in part through imagery. Single words produce images in the mind, as we have seen: river, rose, rain. Images are made more vivid by being specific: a winding river, a red rose, a gentle rain. The image also becomes vital through the use of figures of speech.

A simile is a comparison using "like" or "as."

> Mary had a little lamb,
> Its fleece was white as snow;
> > --Mother Goose

A metaphor is a comparison without the use of "like" or "as" and transforms the comparison into a new entity making a stronger and more immediate image than a simile.

THE SCARLET KEY

> I woke up to a world of white--
> Snow had fallen through the long, still night,
> Locking the world in an eerie spell.
> No color glowed; no sound fell.
> Then a flash of scarlet broke the mood--
> A cardinal in search of food.
> > --Vardine Moore

Personification gives human characteristics to that which is not a person.

THE CLOCK

> There's a neat little clock--
> > In the schoolroom it stands--
> And it points to the time
> > With its two little hands.

> And may we, like the clock,
>   Keep face clean and bright,
> With hands ever ready
>   To do what is right.
>
> --Mother Goose

Onomatopoeia imitates the sound of the word designated. Babies use onomatopoeia after they learn to form words, using the sound that the object makes for the name of the object: Bow-wow, Moo, Choo-choo. Harry Behn tells of a little girl who made up a poem, "Clink, clank, clunk," explaining that it was "carpenters in the sunshine working on a new house and pounding nails" (from "Poetry for Children," Horn Book Magazine, 42, April 1966, pp. 163-175).

Another element for making poetry vital is the use of the senses by which we perceive the world. The poet David McCord advises us to look at one beautiful thing each day in his book Take Sky. There is always the sky in all its various aspects of beauty. Mother Goose rhymes are richer in sight images than in any other.

> I saw a ship a-sailing,
> A-sailing on the sea;
> And, oh! it was all laden
> With pretty things for me!
>
> --Mother Goose

> I see the moon
>   And the moon sees me;
> God bless the moon
>   And God bless me.
>
> --Mother Goose

The sense of hearing comes very early in life, even before seeing, and is found throughout poetry to give added sensory appeal.

> Hark, hark!
> The dogs do bark!
>
> --Mother Goose

> Ride a cockhorse to Banbury Cross,
>   To see a fine lady upon a white horse,
> Rings on her fingers, and bells on her toes,
>   She shall have music wherever she goes.
>
> --Mother Goose

The sense of touch helps us, even as babies, to understand the world.

> I love little Pussy,
>   Her coat is so warm,
> And if I don't hurt her,
>   She'll do me no harm.
>   --Mother Goose

> Four and twenty tailors went to kill a snail,
> The best man among them durst not touch her tail;
> She put out her horns like a little Kyloe cow,
> Run tailors, run, or she'll kill you all e'en now.
>   --Mother Goose

A very popular and frequently used sense is that of tasting. Many mouth-watering examples abound in Mother Goose.

> Curly-locks! Curly-locks! wilt thou be mine?
> Thou shalt not wash dishes nor yet feed the swine;
> But sit on a cushion, and sew a fine seam,
> And feast upon strawberries, sugar and cream!
>   --Mother Goose

> Little Jack Horner sat in the corner,
> Eating his Christmas pie;
> He put in his thumb, and pulled out a plum,
> And said, "What a good boy am I!"
>   --Mother Goose

Closely allied to the sense of taste is the sense of smell.

> The three little kittens washed their mittens, and
> hung them up to dry,
>   "Oh mother dear, look here, look here,
>   Our mittens we have washed!"

> "What! washed your mittens, you darling kittens!
>   But I smell a rat close by!
>   Hush! hush! hush!
>   --Mother Goose

In addition to these five senses, other senses are alert in the awareness of the poet. A sense of wonder is evident in this verse:

Twinkle, twinkle, little star!
How I wonder what you are,
Up above the world so high,
Like a diamond in the sky.
                    --Often attributed to Mother Goose,
                    but actually written by Ann and
                    Jane Taylor

SUDDEN WINGS

A flock of birds on a quiet fence!
Each bird like a lump o' gray-brown clay!
With a rocketing rush of sudden wings,
In one swift arc, they billowed away.

What was the signal?
Who said the word?
I wonder which one was the leader bird.
                    --Vardine Moore

A sense of humor adds fun to poetry, for both the
reader and the writer.

THE MAN IN THE WILDERNESS

The man in the wilderness asked me
How many strawberries grew in the sea.
I answered him as I thought good,
As many as red herrings grew in the wood.
                    --Mother Goose

THE KILKENNY CATS

There were once two cats of Kilkenny,
Each thought there was one cat too many;
So they fought and they fit,
And they scratched and they bit,
    Till, excepting their nails
    And the tips of their tails,
Instead of two cats, there weren't any.
                    --Mother Goose

While there is no final, once-and-for-all definition of
poetry, there are sub-definitions acceptable to everyone and
necessarily understood by anyone interested in poetry.   The
terms "poetry" and "verse" are often used interchangeably;
the word "verse" originally meant, and can still mean, a

single metric line divided into feet. It has come to mean
metric composition as distinguished from prose. More
loosely used, it means the lighter forms of poetry in stanza
form.

The word "stanza," also used interchangeably with
the word "verse," is one or more lines constituting a division of a poem or verse. It corresponds to a paragraph in
prose, and it indicates a formalized unit of a poem.

The study of techniques is not merely an end in itself,
but is presented here in very simple terms to increase the
understanding and delight in appreciation and in participation
when exploring poetry with children.

Much poetry and verse fails because of ignorance of
the basic fundamentals of good versification, just as knowledge of techniques is important in all the fine arts, including music, painting, sculpture, drama and dancing.

The joy of poetry is intensified by awareness of what
poetry is. Robert Frost compares the growth of appreciation to the movement of a pebble cast into water, flowing
outward in ever-increasing circles.

Chapter 3

KEEPING THE SPARK ALIVE

Young children come to school essentially poetic
human beings. However, during the beginning years, the
creative spark begins to flicker feebly and, lacking nourishment, threatens to fizzle out entirely. Spontaneous, original
expression diminishes in frequency and quality, which is
not surprising when we consider the probable causes.

Starting school is a dramatic and sometimes traumatic
experience in a child's life; new disciplines to cope with,
time schedules to meet, new skills to learn, and the adjust-
ment to strangers both peer and adult. The need for conformity tends to mold thought and action. No daydreaming,
no looking out the windows are necessary admonitions. Children also frequently become fearful of being creative and
feel obliged to cater to what they think adults want.

In learning to read and write, there is a shift in
attention from hearing the spoken word to deciphering written
symbols for sound. The process is difficult, often quench-
ing the enjoyment of words and growth of vocabulary. In
spite of facing the enormous responsibility of teaching basic
mechanical skills, almost all teachers made an admirable
effort to keep interest in poetry alive through nursery rhymes
and appropriate verse as the occasion arises and time allows.
Creative teachers are also interested in recognizing and
encouraging creative expression from the children. There
is also a great wave of poetry programs in progressive
schools.

At home and in the library, there is a challenging opportunity to share poetry with, by, and for children and to give them even more exposure to this art form. This is particularly important when there is little or no time in the school day for poetry appreciation.

In talking with a first grader, I asked, "Do you have poetry in school?" She then asked me, "What is poetry?" I tried to explain without going into many possible definitions that it was something like a song, only spoken instead of sung. To which she replied, "Oh, we haven't come that far yet." When I asked her if she knew "Jack and Jill went up the hill," her eyes danced. "Of course."

She proved it by reciting both stanzas and several other familiar Mother Goose favorites, then added several jingles from TV and radio commercials, repeating over and over, "It tastes yummy in your tummy," obviously delighted with the rhyme and rhythm.

Advertisers, political campaign managers, and athletic cheering sections know the value of verse for catching on quickly, arousing enthusiasm, stimulating the imagination, and becoming imprinted indelibly on the mind. The distinguished writer John Ciardi, whose poetry has great appeal --some for children, some for adults and some for both alike--says that rhythm makes the poem dance; rhyme makes it easy to remember.

Verses learned at home, at school, and in the library become a life-long part of our lives. My mother remembered United States capitals from jingles learned in school and relished reciting them to her grandchildren: "Maine, Augusta is on the Kennebec River, Vermont, Montpelier is on the Winooski River." And so on.

How often we use rhymes learned in our youth to remember important information! "Thirty days hath September, April, June and November. All the rest have thirty-one, except February alone, which has twenty-eight in fine-- and in Leap Year, twenty-nine." No one can ever forget the date of Columbus's voyage who has learned the rhyme, "In fourteen hundred ninety-two/Columbus sailed the ocean blue." Our minds hold a store of verses and poems, important and unimportant, learned at home from TV, radio and poetry-loving adults, at school from interested teachers, and from the library with its rich offering of books.

Libraries are not just for books anymore. Modern
libraries--urban, suburban and rural--have been branching
out into areas of service once unheard of. In addition to
using the latest periodicals and reference material, you may
use your card to borrow not only books, but pictures, tools,
films, tapes, phonograph records, even games for your children.

In pleasant surroundings, with carpeting, fireplaces
and gardens in some places, you may use copying machines,
enjoy paintings, exhibits, and specialized programs ranging
from story-telling hours for your children to study groups
for all ages. You may reserve rooms for special events
sponsored by your group.

It should not be difficult to find someone to be in
charge of a poetry group, club or class, whatever it may
be called. This person does not need to be a published or
even practicing poet, but one who understands the basic
qualities of poetry, enjoys reading it and enjoys working
with children. There may be someone on the staff who has
the urge to linger over shelving poetry books and who eagerly
scans new ones that have just arrived, who, indeed, might
welcome the chance to work with children and poetry. Or
there may be a patron who is noticed gravitating to the
poetry books on every visit to the library and never leaves
without a goodly number. Such individuals usually have a
natural desire to share their love of poetry and a flair for
kindling enthusiasm. Children respond eagerly to this
warmth and interest. To find a leader, ask around. This
challenge is not likely to be ignored.

For years, many libraries have offered after-school
activities appealing to children: story hours, Great Books
courses, crafts, movies, Fun and Games, etc. More and
more libraries are offering creative writing groups. We
began such an experiment at the Evansville Public Library
with an invitation "to boys and girls from 5th grade through
the 8th grade to join the Creative Writing Club which will
meet on Friday afternoons at 3:30 in the children's room at
the Central Library." Notice was given by posters in the
library, school newsletters, and by word of mouth to child
and adult patrons. The registration sheet at the check-out
desk was soon overflowing with names of boys and girls.

We began with an eight-week summer session and
continued with sessions through the fall, winter and spring.

The project was extended to branch libraries as interest
grew. To our surprise, a scattering of 4th graders, even
an occasional 2nd and 3rd grader showed up on the first
meeting day, with pencils and notebooks, eager and confident.

There is no lack of ideas in the minds of these
younger ones; they know what they want to say, but are
sometimes intimidated by the older, more sophisticated children who are more proficient in the mechanics of getting
their thoughts down on paper. The thoughts of the less
mature become blocked by stopping to ask, "Do you want
me to print or write?" or they feel compelled to ask how
to spell words they wish to use. In order to capture the
moment of inspiration, I may assure them, "It doesn't really
matter now. Just write in the way you feel most comfortable. We can polish later. All poets try to make their
poems better by going over them after the first try. That's
part of the fun." Another way of relieving anxiety is to
ask, "Would you like to tell me your poem and have me
write it down for you?" There is also the problem that
poems chosen for sharing with the children may not all have
the same appeal for all ages.

It would be better to divide the age groups when
possible into two weekly sessions or into alternating courses
for the older and younger. Sessions for the early grades
may be better attended since there are fewer competing
after-school activities, such as paper routes, athletic programs, piano lessons, school meetings, etc. , all good in
themselves.

This difficulty in making choices is expressed by a
7th grader in a note left for me in the library:

> Dear Mrs. Moore and Writing Friends,
>   I am sorry but I will not be able to attend any
> further meetings until "Volley Ball Season" is
> over, since I am a member of the team this year,
> or at least a sub. Because of this I will have to
> attend all practices including Fridays.
>   I will send my poems to you, Mrs. Moore, so
> you can correct them.
>   Thank you for the pleasure of attending the club.
>   I will return.
>   A devoted member,
>   Colleen
> P.S. Please tell Penny I hope she changes her
> mind about Volley Ball.

Penny did not change her mind and Colleen did return after volleyball season.

I wish Colleen had not said "correct" her work, which is, no doubt, a carry-over from school assignments. The purpose of a creative poetry group is not to teach poetry nor to use a red pencil on mistakes in spelling, punctuation and grammar, nor to change the thoughts expressed, but to bring poetry and children together for appreciation and participation.

In this note, another member of the group shows her eagerness to share what she has written:

> Dear Mrs. Moore,
> I won't be able to come this week to the writing club but I will try to come the next week. I have to go to the Park.
> > Sincerely yours,
> > Karen
> P. S.   I sent my poem with Yvonne.   Please let her read it.

It is important to establish a place to meet, which could be a fairly quiet nook or corner, preferably a separate room where possible.   Books of poetry should be easily accessible to savor with the children and to encourage them to dip into independently.   Whether the collection is large or small, there is always a problem in shelving.   Rhyming storybooks such as those by Aileen Fisher are sometimes filed with prose story books; Mother Goose books are not always in the poetry section, but filed separately.   Even poetry books per se, when filed alphabetically, display many levels of interest and reading ability intermingled.   Individual libraries work out the best system to suit their own needs.

One solution would be to place books out on a table in the meeting place, selected according to the age interests of the group meeting at a designated time.   Your poetry table has other possibilities for providing a center of interest.   Possibly placed against a wall, colorful book jackets, a picture, or inviting posters can be hung above.   Varying displays upon the table, changed from time to time, can add further interest: a bowl of flowers or an arrangement of bare twigs, some shiny brass or a figurine, a bit of sculpture, or a collection of seashells--all with sensory appeal, an important ingredient of poetry.

Since the stuff of poetry is not all beauty and sensory impressions, nor all "How do you feel about it?" but equally important "What do you think?" the poems in Valerie Worth's delightful books, Small Poems and More Small Poems suggest other objects for display: a magnifying glass, a magnet, a raw carrot, pins, acorns, pebbles, a jar of caterpillars. Your own imagination and ingenuity will add to the list. A boy once brought a jar of tadpoles to our library group. A mother whose small son makes poems of rare insight helped him fill small jars of colored water to sparkle on a sunny kitchen windowsill at home.

When we read the poems of Valerie Worth, Pablo Neruda, Gwendolyn Brooks and other fine poets whose works appeal to all ages, we are reminded of Miss Brooks' own definition of poetry as "life distilled." The subjects for poetry are not limited.

After the children are welcomed into a friendly, relaxed atmosphere in a comfortable setting with chairs arranged informally--even a rug or scattered pillows encourage a feeling of relaxation--they may want to browse through the books on the table until everybody arrives. Many have beautiful illustrations which may prompt a child who cannot read well to ask to have one read aloud. If there is no such request, I start the ball rolling with, "Here is one I'd like to read to you. I hope you'll like it too."

Poetry is primarily meant to be heard because rhythm and rhyme appeal to the ear more than through the eye. There is magic in listening to poetry: the magic of music, the magic of words, the magic of pictures brought to mind, meanings to be thought about, and the magic of humor to be shared.

We must have a genuine love of poetry ourselves with some ability to read aloud or quote from memory. The poem should be spoken in a natural voice. Speak all the words clearly, enunciating each consonant crisply. Be careful to keep the rhythm or cadence, trying to let the poem flow naturally without stopping at the end of each line and without bumping your nose on a rhyming word. Never stop to explain word meaning or technical points or in any way interfere with the pure enjoyment of the poem. It is better to read it again, perhaps suggesting that the children close their eyes and find what pictures come to mind.

After re-reading a poem, it may be helpful to note
a beautiful phrase, an unusual word or the new use of a
familiar one. If there is discussion, it should be voluntary.
Questions should be answered, but the exact meaning is not
necessary to the enjoyment of a poem.

We all have our favorites; there is an abundance of
poetry both old and new, like a sky full of stars. There
are dozens of new poetry books which appeal to the interests,
diction, and understanding of today's children. It is wise
not to stick entirely to simple forms with a rigid adherence
to age levels. The imagination is stimulated and vocabulary
grows if we do not limit certain poems to specific age groups,
either in language or content.

Whether or not to memorize poetry is a debatable
question. There does not seem to be much advantage in
memorization when it is used as an assignment without choice
or consideration of poems a child really wants to know by
heart. A favorite poem heard again and again will make an
indelible imprint on the mind to last a lifetime as a source
of comfort and pleasure, a talisman in times of loneliness,
boredom or stress. As Beatrice de Regniers says in her
poem from Something Special (Harcourt, 1958): "Keep a
poem in your pocket."

Almost any child is stimulated to be creative by reading poetry or hearing it read aloud. Something cannot come
out of nothing. Wells must be primed, reservoirs filled,
seeds planted, a springboard provided as an incentive to
diving in. The more poems they are involved with, exposed
to, the more they are moved to experiment with their own
rhythms and rhymes, their own creative sources.

One does not worry about the greatness or perfection
of these beginning efforts. An artist knows great joy in the
act of creation and in sharing what comes forth, making us
see what he sees, telling us his thought and what his own
experience brings forth. Withdrawn personalities blossom
under the warmth of approval and acceptance. It is important that children try their wings in an atmosphere of trust,
encouragement and tolerance.

Recognition and comments of a positive nature with
explanations of what constitutes virtues of their offerings
contribute to greater confidence. We must keep in mind
that children are squelched by too much direction or by

having none.   Too much praise makes children want to please adults and forces expressions that may have nothing to do with the child's own true feelings.   When told a poem, write it down; comment, "I like the way you said that."

At the close of each library session the best poems written during that period are selected by the members to be printed in a booklet with a brightly colored cover or a broadside, which is a large sheet of paper printed on one or both sides used after short terms when there are fewer poems to select from.   These presentations are prepared in the library office for distribution to the children, to schools and throughout the library system.

For this book, I have chosen as examples the best poems written by children from hundreds I have collected, hoping that those who lag far behind in their efforts will someday catch up to those who express their thoughts and feelings easily and naturally in cadence and rhythm, unforced rhyme, imagery, form and other qualities of good poetry. At least, they will all be exposed to poetry and some will continue to grow in their creative efforts, while all will be able to appreciate and enjoy what others have written.

Chapter 4

FANNING THE SPARK

The pre-schooler's delight in Mother Goose and other nursery rhymes carries over into kindergarten and primary grades. It is a good plan, then, to begin with this age group by sharing selections they know and enjoy. This experience is like meeting an old friend in new and unfamiliar surroundings.

The charm of verbal content and the musical quality of old rhymes continue to bring enthusiastic response as we move on to chants, jingles, rhyming riddles and tongue twisters dear to the hearts of children. Excellent source books include A Rocket in My Pocket, a collection of more than four hundred rhymes and chants by Carol Withers; Juba This and Juba That, selections by Virginia A. Tashjian; and Sally Go Round the Sun, collected by Edith Fowka.

It is an easy and natural step to introduce poets of childhood, both traditional and contemporary, from this partial list:

Dorothy Aldis
Harry Behn
William Blake
Gwendolyn Brooks
Margaret Wise Brown
Lewis Carroll
Marchette Chute
John Ciardi

Elizabeth Coatsworth
Walter de la Mare
Paul Lawrence Dunbar
Ivy O. Eastwick
Eleanor Farjeon
Eugene Field
Aileen Fisher
Rose Fyleman

Edward Lear
Vachel Lindsay
Myra Cohn Livingston
David McCord
Eve Merriam
A. A. Milne
Laura E. Richards
James Whitcomb Riley

Elizabeth Madox Roberts
Christina Rossetti
Carl Sandburg
Robert Louis Stevenson
James S. Tippett
Winifred Welles
Valerie Worth
Annette Wynne

There is often a spontaneous feedback of original poems from children after they have listened to a variety of good poetry. These ventures may be spoken as the adult writes them down, or they may be directed into a tape recorder for possible revision and improvement afterward. Children understand and enjoy polishing first efforts; it is always possible to find something good in the children's work and encourage them to develop it further.

The important thing is getting started. However, in any group there are children who simply blank out or feel shy about making an individual effort. In this case, group poems are valuable and are often set into motion by one of the class members. Thomas, a self-starter, set the ball rolling one day by a chant in the familiar rhythm of "She'll Be Coming Round the Mountain."

> I wish I were a horse--neigh, neigh.
> I wish I were a horse--neigh, neigh.
> I would eat all the hay,
> And then I'd play croquet.
> Oh, I wish I were a horse--neigh, neigh.
>
> I wish I were a gator in a swamp--swish, swish.
> I wish I were a gator in a swamp--swish, swish.
> I'd catch a little fish
> And serve him on a dish.
> Oh, I wish I were a gator in a swamp--swish, swish.
>   -- Thomas Goodloe

Soon others in the class were rolling along with stanzas of their own:

> I wish I were a pig--oink, oink.
> I wish I were a pig--oink, oink.
> If I were a pig,
> I would dance a little jig.

Oh, I wish I were a pig--oink, oink.
                    --Kimberly Grigsby

I wish I were a dog--woof, woof.
I wish I were a dog--woof, woof.
If I were a dog,
I would chase a hopping frog.
Oh, I wish I were a dog--woof, woof.
                    --Teri Darrington

I wish I were a mosquito--bite, bite.
I wish I were a mosquito--bite, bite.
I would bite into your skin,
Like a big sharp pin.
I wish I were a mosquito--bite, bite.
                    --Scott Kirves

I wish I were the rain--splish, splash.
I wish I were the rain--splish, splash.
I would splatter on the grass,
And make rivers down the glass.
Oh, I wish I were the rain--splish, splash.
                    --James Clardy

I wish I were a little piece of hay--crunch, crunch.
I wish I were a little piece of hay--crunch, crunch.
I would scatter all around
And I wouldn't make a sound.
Oh, I wish I were a little piece of hay--crunch,
crunch.
                    --Jenny Woodworth

I wish I were a plane--zoom, zoom.
I wish I were a plane--zoom, zoom.
I would fly through the air
And I wouldn't have a care.
Oh, I wish I were a plane--zoom, zoom.
                    --Kenneth Clardy

    Scott, a third-grader, gave a springboard to the group
with nonsense rhymes in couplets, which inspired a wave of
original rhymes:

        Poodles are noodles
        At Georgie McSnoodles.
                    --Scott Kirves

Turtles ate girdles
At Miss McFurtles.

                    --Kenneth Pferrer

A gorilla drank sasparilla
At Mrs. Farilla's.

                    --Shawn Williams

The foxes ate boxes
At Mr. Foloxes.

                    --Elizabeth Miley

Rabbits had bad habits
At Miss McGabbits.

                    --Thomas Goodloe

A hog ate a dog
At Mrs. McLog's.

                    --Philip Goodloe

In the Fine Arts Program for children at the University of Evansville, members of the creative poetry class offered to write lyrics for music composed by a class of music theory. Sister Mary Inez Mitchell, the music teacher, had directed her class in a creative composition entitled "A Lazy Summer Afternoon" in ABA form in four-four time.

Using the music as a guide, the class developed a poem in triplet form and, working as a group, found words and meaning appropriate to the title. The composition on the following page was performed in a program for the entire school.

When there is no voluntary inspiration, the group quickly becomes involved in discussions of some interest mentioned by one of the children; animals and pets, families and adventure or emotional experience, even dreams and nightmares.

Animals and pets are popular subjects and bring a variety of individual contributions:

My horse is red and brown
His mane is like silk.
His ears stand up
When you call him.

A LAZY SUMMER AFTERNOON

We went walking
Down along the shady pathway
Underneath the trees.

Hand in hand we
Strolled beside the flowing river
Catching each cool breeze.

Suddenly we
Saw a rowboat
Tied close by.

We stepped on and
Dipped our toes into the water
Gazing at the sky.

John Cooper
Angela Gallagher
Deanna Gallagher
Eric Helmbock
Melissa Seib

Shara Sights
Michael Schmidt
Ryan Serber
Benjy Spillman
Lisa Gelhausen

He gallops like the winds
And I like to brush him.

--Mark Alcott

Whether this was a real horse or one in his imagination, I never asked. It really doesn't matter; the poem does.
There is no need to analyze or criticize. It is sufficient to
say, "I like that." Or, since there is imagery ("He gallops
like the wind"), "You made us see that."

LAUGHING TIME

The monkey from the high, high tree
Started laughing hee, hee, hee.
The donkey everybody saw
Started laughing haw, haw, haw,
Then the pony eating hay
Started laughing neigh, neigh, neigh.

--Andrea Klinger

OUR DOG JAM

We went to pick raspberries
But they were all picked out.
We found a puppy instead.
We called it Jam for two reasons:
One--we went to get berries for jam.
Two--our father and mother would be
     in a jam.

--Thomas Goodloe

THE TURTLE

He walked around with stretched up neck,
Not really looking where he was going.
He tried to climb my mother's leg,
And made her drop her sewing.

--Scott Kirves

POOR LITTLE POODLE

There was a French poodle;
Her name was Noodle.
She wore red polish on every nail.
On her head she carried a pail.
Her feet were in pain-
Poor little dog.
It began to rain.

The milk in the pail turned clear.
Poor little dog.
The market place was very near
But she had lost the sale
Of the milk in the pail.

--Jennie Woodworth

LONG AGO
When I look out my window,
I wish I could see buffalo.
Buffalo used to roam
On land that is now my home.

--Joe Elliott

LITTLE FROG IN THE FOREST

Down in the forest so deep, so deep
Down in the forest, where no one would peep,
Down in the grass,
Down in the sand,
   A little frog jumps
      Like a fat rubber band.

--Scott Kirves

I like Alligators
that live in the slimy swamp,
slithering and sliding,
swimming in the solitary silence.

--Heather Himebaugh

HONEY BEES

I like flowers, I like trees,
I like busy little honey bees
Buzzing on a day that's sunny
gathering nectar for their honey.

--Leann Cox

Although it is difficult to be original in poems of the
seasons and nature, children often express personal views
with grace and insight.

LATE SNOW

Snow on the leaves
And a little breeze
Form a silver Spring.

--Kim Ewing

THE FIR TREE

Our fir tree stands tall,
Not small, at all.
Its branches stand out
As if it wanted to touch our house.
And as I watch out our window,
I can see
The beautiful snowflakes sprinkling our tree.

--Cheryl Martin

TRACKS IN THE SNOW

Snow, Snow, my beautiful snow!
They have tracked it all up!
How dare they!
The bird tracks aren't so bad.
But the dog tracks, the cat tracks,
The foot tracks, the tire tracks ...
O, my beautiful snow!

--Cheryl Martin

SNOW CANDY

Marshmallows
On the brown fence post
Look good enough to eat.

But if you ever eat one
It will drip, drip, drip
Down to your feet.

--Robert Fleming

THE RAIN POND

After a spring shower
We walked through the field
To a rain pond.
We scooped up a big crawdad in a bucket.
Well--maybe a craw-mommy
With a sack of babies attached.
In the night it had fourteen tiny crawdads.
Well--maybe craw-babies.
I fished one out on my finger tip.
He was so little.
He was born last night in a bucket.
I put him in a paper cup

With a rock to hide under.
He was so little.

                              --Thomas Goodloe

MARCH WINDS

Ribbons of dust
Rolling up and down the street,
Pushing bits of dried up leaves
    All around my feet!

I don't like the March winds,
I prefer the April rain,
Because, soon after,
    Spring flowers come again.

                              --Lynn Trockman

WARM SPRING DAY

What can I do on a warm spring day?
    "Go on a picnic," suggested my mother.
    "Or just go away," complained my dad.
"Go look for a bird's egg,
But don't break your leg.
Go pick some flowers to put in a vase,
Or go swimming in one of the bays.
The water is nice and cool,
Better than a pool."
    So what can you do on a warm spring day?
    Anything!   Just go away.

                              --Lisa Klinger

ONE WINDY DAY

One windy day
In the month of March,
Hats were blowing,
Roosters were crowing,
Everything was chaos.

The wind was howling,
Parents were scowling.
Kids were having fun.
Helping everyone
Gather up their hats.

                              --Cheryl Martin

While raking the newly cut grass,
I hate that.
The cut grass covers
The growing grass
Like a blanket.

--Kim Ewing

SUNDOWN

Tell the crew
  The gardening's through.
  The weeding, the hoeing,
  We're through with you.
  We've quit for the day.
  Hip, hip, Hurray!

--Thomas Goodloe

HALLOWEEN

Halloween is the time
We go Halloweening
And see pumpkins in the windows.
They grin at me.

But I don't scare.
I grin right back
And walk up to the door.
I yell "Trick or Treat!"
It's Halloween.   -- Bob Kluger

Poems which reflect emotional experiences and meaningful observations are among the best poems written by
children. These poems reveal thoughts and feelings of the
writers about themselves and the world around them.

HELLO WORLD

I climb a Tower,
  Hello World
  I see a flower,
    Hello World
    I climb down
      The tower,
Hello World
I smell the flower.

--Joe Elliott

FISHING

There is a boy
Who lives in the city.
He came to visit us in the country.
He caught four fish
Out of our lake.
And I didn't catch a one!

--Shara Sights

STORES

When you go to the store,
They don't greet you at the door.
But they're glad
Because you saw their newspaper ad.
They want you to buy their stuff,
But that's not enough
When you go to the store,
They should greet you at the door.

--Joe Elliott

ME

My name is Scott.
I'm a silver sandpiper
Sliding on the silky sea.

I'm a spring singer.
I see sandy salamanders
Sliding on the silky sea.

I saw Sandy Seal.
I seem to be in the sky,
But still, I'm just me.

--Scott Kirves

THE LOLLIPOP SONG

Slurp, slurp, slurp.
Sl-l-l-l-l-lurp.
Piddle-lump, piddle-lump.
My favorite flavor
Is grape and orange mixed.
All put together into one big swirl.

--Jackie Ewing

Once on the way to school
I met a bully.
He beat me up.
But the next time
I went a different way.

--Kristin Rusche

When I feel mean and don't want to go home,
I feel rotten and tired to the bone.
I just kick a stone, a stone.

When I walk home from school alone,
I feel lonesome and not even known.
I just kick a stone, a stone.

I finally get home and start to the door,
I hear my friends call--I'm not sore anymore.
So I don't kick a stone, a stone.

--Scott Kirves

The following poems followed a group discussion on
"What I want to be when I grow up."

When I grow up
I'm going to be a dentist.
I'm going to take care
Of children's teeth.
I'm going to x-ray their teeth
They can read magazines
While I fix the x-rays.

I'm going to count their teeth
And clean their teeth
Then they can pick out a toy
From the toy box.

--Carolyn Martin

DOCTOR FIRST

When I grow up I'm going to be
         A doctor
         And operate.
For doctors, you know,
         They operate
         And do surgery.

They dig in your tummy

And give you good pills.
    And that is how
    They cure all your ills.
So to school I'll go
And learn to be a doctor.

They say it's fun to be
    A business man
    Or a garbage man
And empty every can.
But still I'd rather be
A nice, handsome doctor.
    That's what I'm going to be
    And
      You
        Can't
          Change
            My
            Mind!

                        --Fred Creech

     Imagination is a vital factor in a child's approach to creative writing. After a visit to a nearby exhibit of driftwood art, the following poems were written.

THE IMAGINNAIRE MAN

The ruffled stallion hanging from the wall,
His mane flying in the wind.
He looks like striking booms of wind.
I love the driftwood stallion.

                        --Robert Fleming

THE LAUGHING PORPOISE

See the happy porpoise,
See him leaping in the air.
He is made of driftwood,
Polished, scrubbed and shiny.
It makes me happy
To see the laughing porpoise.

                        --Elizabeth Miley

THE STALLION

The wild stallion,
Separated from the stampede,

His mane flying in the air,
Is trying to find his lost band.

                    --David Pannkuk

WOOD WORM

I like the wood worm
best of all
Creeping, eating,
Grinding slowly through.

                    --Thomas Goodloe

DRIFTWOOD ART

All shapes of driftwood
Drifted in from the river.
Nature formed the shapes,
Beasts and birds and fish.
Art recognized by man.

                    --Elizabeth Miley

DYING TURTLE

Driftwood on the beach,
Sculptured by the wind and waves.
Old rotten turtle.

                    --Thomas Goodloe

Telling a story is a natural instinct in children.
Narrative poems may be real or imaginative.

SQUEAKY THE MOUSE

Squeaky was a mouse
Who lived in a grand house.
He lived in a hole in the kitchen
Where the cat was just itchin' to eat him.

Squeaky's life was far from dull.
Do you know why?
He got caught in a mouse trap
While flipping pancakes in the sky.

There was one thing to do.
Get out of there.
So he packed a tooth brush
And a brush for his hair.

"Now," said Squeaky,
Determined and grim,
"Can you help me out of here?"
Children, can you help him?

                              --Mark Seib

NOAH

When Noah built his ark,
He thought he might meet a shark.

It was a heck of a job for a man 500 years old
But Noah was bold.

When the rains came,
The animals were tame.

When the rain came to a stop,
Noah's boat was stuck on a mountain top.

                              --Joe Elliott

A GOAT

A little goat
(So I was told)
Broke loose and ran away.
If he had listened to his mother's warning,
It wouldn't have happened this way.

He met a fox down in the wood,
And he was quite polite.
But the fox down deep was mean,
A very evil sight.

He led the goat straight to a stream
And showed him how to swim.
But then he jumped the little goat
To tear him limb from limb.

But Mother Goat had looked and looked
And found he'd gone astray.
And so she kicked the big fat fox
And sent him on his way.

                              --Scott Kirves

Writing poetry can be a playful pursuit and often
should be. Nonsense rhyme may spring up unexpectedly

without any preliminary groundwork, but simply as an expression of high spirits and an urge to laugh. Laughter is contagious and children join readily in a hilarious session of romping with words.

> A goose is on the loose,
> His name is Little Soose.
> Soose has some brothers,
> But don't tell the others
> That Soose is on the loose.
>
> --John Wittenbraker

ICE CREAM ANNIE

> Ice Cream Annie
> Sitting on her fanny,
> Thinking of how it was
> When she had plenty of ice cream.
>
> Apple, berry,
> Lemon, cherry.
>
> When they returned,
> She was taken by surprise
> And feasted her eyes
> Upon
>
> Apple, berry,
> Lemon, cherry.
>
> --Danny Baker

> Bozo is a mean old dog.
> A dinosaur bit Bozo's leg off.
> He was hungry.
> Crunch, crunch, crunch.
>
> --Patrick McMillan

One little girl commented, "That's a horrible, gorrible, scorrible poem."

SAD STORY OF AN ELEPHANT

> There once was an elephant
> Who thought he was elegant.
>
> His name was Tom,
> He was shaped like a bomb.

He started to climb
A tree thin as a dime.

And when he fell,
He hit a bell.

The bell rang
With a terrible twang.

And Tom,
Like a bomb,
Blew up in the sky,
Very, very, very high.

                              --Joe Elliott

Occasionally a child will complain, "I con't think of anything to write about." Creative writing cannot be forced; inspiration must come effortlessly. Concentration will not help, nor grim determination. Instead of coaxing the child, keep trying to think of something. It is better to say, "That's all right. Let's just talk."

A smile creeps into the dejected face; eyes begin to light up. The incentive to capture an experience and put it into words is most often that of sharing it with someone else.

It is said that the poet William Butler Yeats wrote his poems first in prose. When a little happening unfolds, suggest that the child write it down. "That's interesting. You might make a poem of it."

Following this procedure, the child discovers a rhythm, imagery, often rhymes. With a little help in arranging the lines to give form to the whole, the child is surprised and elated by the result. Kari told me something she had seen and first wrote it out in prose: "On Weinbach street there is an insurance firm. On the letter U of the word: IN-SURANCE, there is a bird nest." The result was a polished poem:

I saw a bird's nest
On Weinbach street.
It was constructed on a sign
That said INSURANCE.

There in the U

The bird had made a home
Unafraid of people and traffic
And storms and prowling cats.
                                        --Kari Points

Another experience was first written in prose: "Steffi
and I were going to class. Along the path a squirrel sat
on the lowest branch of a tree. We stared at her for a
minute. I reached out and petted her. She scampered up
the tree, watching Steffi and me." An interesting poem took
the following form:

SQUIRREL

Steffi and I
Were going to class.

In a tree
Along the path,
A squirrel sat on the lowest branch.

We stared at her for a moment.

I reached up to pet her.
She scampered up the tree,
Watching Steffi and me.
                                        --Kari Points

Lori's recital needed little change:

I saw a locust coming out of his shell.
I knew he wasn't afraid of me
But he didn't move an inch.
He looked green and plastic,
But I knew he was real.
Because all of a sudden
He flew away, leaving his shell on the tree.
                                        --Lori Seiler

These poems by the youngest children in the group
were recorded almost as they were spoken.

THE PARADE

We went to the children's parade.
My sister was in it
Riding on a float.

The clouds were gray
It rained all day.

They put plastic over their heads
But the tapes took off
And they got soaked.

                    --Lauri Schlueter

CLOUDS

The clouds last night were beautiful.
My mom and I went bicycle riding.
We went to get doughnuts.
The clouds looked like doughnuts.

                    --Tashta Matysuk

I saw a lady bug
    Flying
        Flying
            Flying
It landed on my knee
And what did I see!

I saw a lady bug
With only one spot--

A tiny black dot.

                    --Maria Talbert

A statement that rhymes cannot always be called a
finished poem, yet every effort toward poetic expression
should be encouraged. Consider these first attempts as
"five-finger" exercises, as practiced by beginning music
students. The first faltering steps are not ready to be performed at Carnegie Hall and still they can be called music.

A specific topic or theme assigned by an adult for
everyone to fret over simultaneously seldom inspires original expression or honest feeling. The most productive sessions seem to come from suggestions by the children themselves or by their hearing poetry read aloud.

The most important role in nurturing and encouraging
creative expression is to read to the children, to listen to
them, to talk about poetry and, above all, to enjoy sharing
experience with poetry. Richard Lewis, poet, teacher and
collector of children's poems, has noted that the word poetry
in the Eskimo language is also the word that means to breathe.

Chapter 5

THE FLAME BURNS BRIGHTLY

Children in the upper elementary grades have usually reached a higher level of maturity and sophistication, as well as growth in vocabulary, enabling them to handle linguistic skills with greater ease than the younger age. Their thinking is frequently of a more philosophical nature, their feelings inclined toward greater depth and intensity.

Certain children have been in poetry groups before (which accounts for some examples of original poems in this age group by children whose names appeared in the beginning group). There are also new members who have written poems on their own at home or in school classes. When children have experienced writing poetry in any situation, they enter this new encounter eager to read aloud their own previously written work.

This is a good beginning. Hearing poems written by their peers encourages those less secure to make an effort to creative expression of their own. Comments and discussions which follow these readings should be positive rather than negative. Praising fresh imagery, sensory appeal, rhythm and interesting rhyme, well-chosen words and well-turned phrases is a better method of presenting poetry techniques than a long, involved explanation.

No set of rules will be as effective in motivating creative thought as hearing poems by members of the group and by listening to poems from children's anthologies, such

as those by Richard Lewis: Miracles--Poems by Children
of the English Speaking World; There Are Two Lives--Poems
by Children of Japan; and I Breath a New Song--Poems of
the Eskimo.

Many poetry enthusiasts bring books from home or
books checked out from the library shelves to share favorite
poems.   Good poetry read aloud by an adult or one of the
children and listening to poetry recordings provide clues that
suggest new verbal adventures.

Following the reading of "The Great Lover" by Rupert
Brooke and "Barter" by Sara Teasdale, children are inspired
to list their own favorite things.   Children love lists; there
is something definite to catch hold of.   While mere lists
may be something less than pure poetry, the resulting poems
by children are often original and interesting.

THE GREAT LOVER

These things I have loved:
I have loved a warm bed on a cold,
     winter's night,
With the wind howling--
Oh! what a fright;
The flag of our country flying above,
The safety of home and a mother's love;
Snow floating gently to the ground,
Softly, softly without a sound.
These things I have loved.
                                        --Colleen Sharer

MY GREAT LOVES

These things I have loved:
     wood burning in the fireplace
     with smoke circling upward
     to soar away with the birds;
     books which open up a fairyland of wonder;
     a lake shimmering and shining under the
          golden moonlight.
                                        --Melanie Kell

PLEASURES OF LIFE

These are the pleasures of my life:
     the taste of my grandmother's apple pie;

the taste of shrimp,
the feel of the fur on a kitten,
the baa of a goat,
the sound of music,
to see a horse rear up;
and I like to have Daddy fight with me.

--Lillian Faye Cabage

THESE THINGS I HAVE LOVED

My red quilted skirt,
Dotted with tiny, yellow flowers.

The aroma of mashed potatoes
Floating from the kitchen.

The freshness of clean sheets
That feel like satin.

The nightly hug and kiss
From Daddy and Mother.

The hundred on my paper
Written in bright red.

The lovely Christmas angel
Atop the Christmas tree.

--Mary Louise Moutoux

SOUNDS I LIKE

I like these sounds:
    the whinny of a horse,
    the galloping hoofs of a horse,
    the purring of a kitten,
    the bark of a dog,
    my mother's scream when she sees
        scampering, little mice.

--Lillian Cabage

LITTLE THINGS

Little things are fun for me.
Fun to touch and fun to see.
Little dolls in match-box chairs.
Teen, tiny teddy bears;
Tiny fish with silver fins,

Little nails as thin as pins;
Baby shoes, baby mice,
Tiny books as small as stamps,
Thread spools make nice table lamps.
Little things,
I like them.

--Karen Smith

After reading Hailstones and Halibut Bones by Mary O'Neill, the children find a personal reaction to the subject of color.

PINK

Pink is a pretty colored rose.
Pink is the blemish on someone's nose.
Pink is the color of my sister's bike.
Pink is a color I really like.

--Autumn Newsome

BLUE

Blue is a color I like too.
Blue is the color of a cloud.
Blue is a color not very loud.
Blue is the color of you.

--Autumn Newsome

PINK

Pink is a stink
for boys.
Pink is fink
For boys.
PINK IS NUTTY.

Gold is bold

I like gold!

--John Wittenbraker

I LIKE WHITE

White is a wedding dress, long and lacy,
White is a spotted Dalmatian named Tracey.
White is a horse so shiny and silky.
White is cream, rich and milky.

White is a dove,
That reminds me of love.

                                        --Angela Brown

Reading "The End" by A. A. Milne was a springboard
to writing their own biographies.

THE END

When I was one,
I gained a ton.

When I was two,
I could tie my shoe.

When I was three,
I could climb a tree.

When I was four,
I could shut the door.

When I was five,
I could swim and dive.

When I was six,
I could pick up sticks.

When I was seven,
I learned about heaven.

When I was eight,
I learned to skate.

When I was nine,
I could drink wine.

When I was ten,
I did it all over again!

                                        --Suzanne Suhrheinrich

An older member of the group submitted the following:

CHILD PRODIGY

When I was one, I could read and write,
When I was two, I flew a kite.
When I was three, I could spell and do math,
When I was four, I could draw my own bath.

When I was five, I called Mother, Mater,
When I was six, I called Father, Pater.
When I was seven, college work was easy,
And at eight, getting a degree was breezy.
When I was nine, for freedom I yearned,
Now I am ten, there's nothing to be learned.
                                        --Carolyn Sparks

This is also the age group that enjoys talking. The
kind of talk that goes on is often a means of getting acquainted
with each other and leads to sharpening ideas to write about.
As with the younger members of writing groups, familiar
subjects predominate, using a personal approach--families,
animals, nature, experiences and observations feature promi-
nently in their poems which are often colored by deep feeling. Animals and pets are still popular subjects:

PIERROT-HAPPY

With black eyes gleaming, tufted tail aplume,
Pierrot darts here and there,
And the grass sings as his feet
Romp through. He's not aware
Of the joyful picture he makes.
He is smiling--his red tongue is out.
Wind dances through his white fur.
He is so happy he could almost shout,
"The sun is shining and so am I.
And beautiful is the day."
With a jump, a bark, and a smile,
He gambols his poodle way.
                                        --Graeme Browning

THAT LOOK

There is something in your eyes,
Something that I can't surmise
As to what it's supposed to mean,
I've never seen.
Oh, Pierrot!
Now in your eyes I can see
The fear, surprise
And I read joy
As in a book.
But what, oh what
Is that other look?
                                        --Graeme Browning

KITTENS

Kittens open their
   eyes and look wondering about
      as if to say "WOW!"

                        --Sarah McCray

ANOTHER KIND OF CAT

Kitty-cat
I know you're hungry
For you roam the city streets.
And when the day retreats
And night-time comes,
I know your coat's not thick enough.
But, Kitty-cat
You're a city cat.

                      --Lisa Klinger

MY STALLION AT PLAY

With his neck arched proudly,
His mane whips every way.
His tail is flipped over his back,
His canter is light and gay.
It's my stallion, my stallion,
My blue roan stallion,
My beautiful stallion at play.

He whinnies loudly, joyfully.
He kicks his heels in the air.
He trots, he canters,
He gallops everywhere.
It's my stallion, my stallion,
My blue roan stallion,
My lovely stallion at play.

He rears and paws the air.
Then he turns in flight.
And his tail gives a flick
As he runs out of sight.
It's my stallion, my stallion,
My blue roan stallion,
My regal stallion at play.

                 --Graeme Browning

THE WOLF'S CRY

The moon hangs low in the black night sky,
The trees are black and bare.
Suddenly a wolf howls long and low;
It echoes in the still night air.

Then the howling stops
And all is still,
Till another wolf answers
From over the hill.

Then all the wolves howl
Their long, low cry.
And the weird sound echoes
From far and nigh.

--Lisa Klinger

PRAIRIE WINTER

Winter has set in again,
Harsh and cold and bare.
Winding across the snowy ground,
The footprints of a hare.

Over the wind's loud din,
A lonesome coyote howls.
Crouching beneath a lanky pine,
A cougar screams and growls.

--Suzanne Moutoux

DINOSAURS

Dinosaurs once ruled the earth.
Long ago this was their home.
When the world was very new,
That's when they did roam.

Tyrannosaurus was the king
Of every dinosaur.
To eat and sleep was all his life
Then sleep and eat some more.

Diplodocus was the longest one;
He was sort of slender too.
All he did was stand in swamps
And chew and chew and chew.

Brontosaurus, an eater of plants,
And a very gentle one,
Would stand in swamps and eat the plants
Until the day was done.

Stegosaurus had bony plates
Up and down his back.
And on his tail were four long spikes
For protection when attacked.

Triceratops had three long horns
And a shield behind his head.
He wouldn't run from eaters of meat,
But would charge head-on instead.

Pterosaurs roamed the skies
Over land and sea.
Their wings were very, very big
Compared to little me.

Dinosaurs once ruled the earth,
Long, long ago.
They ruled the earth in majesty
Until they had to go.

                                    --Ann Carpenter

Members of the family come in for their share of
attention.

BABY SISTERS

Baby sisters are always fat,
Baby sisters always fall flat,
They always like to play with a hat.

They also like to play with a bat
But they never get to play with that!
                                    --Trip Browning

LOU

Lou is my sister,
She isn't very tall.
If you don't look close
You may not see her at all.

She had blonde hair

And big blue eyes.
When she grows up
She'll catch lots of guys.

She is funny
And runty,
She is thin
Like a little wren.
She is cute as she can be,
I like her and she likes me.

                              --Vickie Purtzer

PORTIA'S HOUR

Portia's hour
   Is packed with power.
She wields her power
   Like a mighty queen.
Nobody can work
   From six to seven,
That's Portia's hour.

                              --Shelly Cook

WORDS FOR HER

"Monkey" and "Imp"
Are two good words
Especially for her.

But then, too,
"Angel" and "Saint"
Fit her too.

That's my sister, Sweet Pea.

                              --Susie Rusche

LOWRY

She's naturally born rude.
She runs around nude
After her bath with Trip.
She gives everyone "the lip"
When she's having a fit.
But that's not it!
She can be sugar and honey
When she wants money.
And in the afternoon

Whoops like a baboon
When she's running with Largo and Trip.
Then gives everyone "the lip"
When she's having a fit.
That's Lowry.

--Graeme Browning

BABIES

A baby,
Well maybe,
Will eat horse food for breakfast,
And pig's food for lunch,
And maybe for brunch,
They'll have something with crunch.
A baby,
Well maybe,
I really can't say
What a baby will eat
Almost any old day.

--Andrea Klinger

TO MY FATHER

We're not the only ones lonesome for you.
I know, yes, I know that Skip is too.
Whenever the door is opened,
He's excited as can be.
But when it's not you
He comes and lies by me.

He's always lying in your chair;
I know he wishes you were there.

This poem I wrote for you,
And every bit of it is true.

--Nan Diekmann

MY GRANDPA'S FALSE TEETH

My grandpa's teeth are funny
   Although they're pearly white.
My grandpa's teeth are different
   'Cause he takes them out at night.
My grandpa takes his teeth out
   When he gets into bed.

I simply sleep with all my teeth
 Safe inside my head.

--Judy Shepard

As with all groups, nature and the seasons provide a
rich variety of subjects and forms.

A HAIKU

Snow on Valentine's
Gives the world a frosty treat
And a lacy look.

--Susie Rusche

WINTER SCENE

A soft quilt of snow
 covers the ground.
The snow weighs down the limbs
 of a birch tree.
Bird seed scattered on the snow,
A snowman in the front yard,
Icicles hanging from the roof,
Children on sleds,
Dogs on a chase
Make our yard a winterplace.

--Pam Ewing

WINTER COMES

The wind howls,
The hoot of the owls,

Snow sliding down the windowpane,
Footprints deeply printed in the lane,

Sleds on hills,
Colds and pills,

Tingling air,
Hibernating bear.

It's then I know that winter comes.

--Suzanne Moutoux

IN BETHLEHEM

I saw the Saviour being born

in Bethlehem,
   I did.

I saw the shepherds come a-down
   in Bethlehem.
      I did.

I saw the wise men and their gifts,
I saw the sheep and ox in bliss.
I saw these things, these wondrous things
   in Bethlehem
      I did!   I did!
                                    --Mary Hughes

THE NIGHT AFTER CHRISTMAS

"Twas the night after Christmas
And all through the house,
Not a creature was stirring
'Cept Herbert's white mouse,
A present to him from his Uncle Guboon.
A gift, said his mother, they'd get rid of soon.

The tree stood in a corner, ornaments askew.
Underneath, shattered remains of toys once new.
The stockings were stuffed with chewed candy and
      peels.
The floor looked as if squirrels had enjoyed their
      meals.
The children were sleeping, one sock off and one
      on,
Betty clutching a new well-chewed fawn.
And Santa, the merry, the jolly old elf,
Well--you can be sure he was in bed himself.
                                    --Penny Moore

THE DIFFERENCE IN DAYS

Spring is coming
And the days stay long enough
To have a cup of tea,
Just dropping in.
When summer comes,
The day will stay
All day.

Spring is coming I know,
Because the day stays

Just long enough to have a cup of tea and chat,
In winter the day
Doesn't do that.
When summer comes,
The day will stay
All day.

                                        --Lisa Klinger

THE PEAR TREE

Every year when spring rolls round,
The pear tree starts to bloom.
First she dons her frilly gown
And holds her green corsage.

Oh, how I dread the fall
When my tree begins to fade.
She closes in her green corsage
And bids her last farewell.

But then I think of spring again
And then of my dear tree,
For I know she'll be back in bloom
Again, again in spring.

                                        --Jean Coyle

SPRING IS ACCIDENTS

My brother got a butterfly lip
Playing ball,
Another five stitches.

I've been fishing twice,
And I have poison ivy.

                                        --Carolyn Johnson

WARM SPRING DAY

What can I do on a warm spring day?
    "Go on a picnic," suggested my mother.
    "Or just go away," complained my dad.
"Go look for a bird's egg
But don't break your leg.
Go pick some flowers to put in a vase,
Or go swimming in one of the bays.
The water is nice and cool,

Better than a pool."
So what can you do on a warm spring day?
Anything!   Just go away.

                              --Lisa Klinger

SPRING

Golden days and cloud-filled skies,
Pretty, soft blue butterflies,
The robin with its bright red vest,
I think I like these days the best.

Silvery days with hazy showers
Bead the faces of the flowers.
Little crawling, creeping things
Find a miracle of wings.

Honeysuckle-scented nights,
Fireflies signalling their flights,
Bashful moon behind the trees,
Spring is author of all these.

                              --Susan McKinney

SUMMER

When it gets hot
The lake dries up.

We have sunflowers
That grow higher than my mom.
I break open the seed
And eat the inside.

                              --Jackie Ewing

IN SUMMERTIME

When the evening sun is setting
And the haze is mystic gold,
We play around in our front yard
With friends both young and old.

We swim all day in summer,
And eat watermelon at night.
The lightning bugs are plenty,
But they never bite.

                              --Lynn Trockman

WHAT IS HALLOWE'EN?

Witches with brooms
Come out to play,
Goblins and cats
Hunting for prey.

You might get scared right out of your wits
By a funny old ghost eating hominy grits.

--Carolyn Johnson

HALLOWE'EN

Spooks and candy--
What a mix!
It sometimes gets you
In a fix.

--Ruth Linstromberg

THE WIND

Over the ocean
The wind howls.
In a far-off valley,
The wind howls.
In big city streets
The wind howls.
But
In my garden, it plays!

--Bruce Kell

WHAT IS THE WIND?

The wind is invisible
Although it can be seen
Through a rippling brook,
Through a rustling tree.

It can be a gale
Fierce and strong.
It can be a breeze
Sailing along.

It can be a tornado
Whirling by.
It can be a hurricane--
It can be a sigh.

--Ann Carpenter

THE LEAF

Once I was a leaf
Hanging from a tree,
Then came the wind
And blew me from that tree.

Then came the winter
That froze me stiff as a twig.
Now I am soil
And not a leaf any more.

--Bruce Kell

These children need not be given specific topics for
starters, but seem to express naturally a compelling thought
or conviction, or personal observation.

A HAIKU

I am beating on
my pillow so I can go
to sleep peacefully.

--John Wittenbraker

LOVE OR DESSERT

I guess when they dished out love
They thought I'd had enough
Of everything else
And was full.
But that's not true,
And if I ever eat there again,
I'm not taking anything
Until the love is passed around,
And then I'll take a second helping.

--Lisa Klinger

BUSY PEOPLE

Hurry, hurry, hurry!
   Scurry, scurry, scurry!
That's all older people do.

Hustle, hustle, hustle!
   Bustle, bustle, bustle!
I don't like it, do you?

--Becky Underwood

DRIFTWOOD

Once a piece of driftwood came floating down the
    river.
It looked like a rabbit on skis.

A parade of animals came floating after it;
Bears, tigers, elephants and fleas.
                                    --Bruce Kell

TREASURES

I can find a wind, light and airy,
I can find a beautiful little fairy,
I can find a mischievous elf.
These are easy to find on a bookshelf.
                                    --Sarah McCray

CEILINGS AND FLOORS

I'm interested in ceilings and floors.
I find them exciting like windows and doors.
We need floors for us to walk on
Like telephones for us to talk on.
We need ceilings to cover our heads
As we need blankets to cover our beds.
We need doors to enter in--
I think to windows, they are kin.
                                    --Judy Shepard

CURLICUES

Some Curlicues are short and fat,
Some are shaped like a great tall hat.
They are seen on marble floors--
They are carved on wooden doors.

Make them out of clay or gold,
People like them--young or old.
I make them on my spelling book,
But Teacher gives me an ominous look.
                                    --Barbara Martin

A BLACKBOARD

A blackboard is used for many things,
For Math   For English   For Spelling, too.

For Geography   For Handwriting   For People's
    names, too.

That's what blackboards are used for.

But there are some more:
For poems   For Games   For Sentences.
So many things you put on blackboards.
                              --Nancy Purtzer

WEEPING WILLOW

As I sit beneath the willow tree,
I ask it why it weeps.
The wind blows its branches
Encircling my feet.
Now, I feel that I am a tree--
My branches bear leaves
That weight my branches down.
My branches and leaves move with the wind.
My roots give me water and food,
But I have no feet.
I am rooted in the ground and cannot move.
Now, Willow, I weep.
I long for movement,
The countryside beckons.
I cannot go,
Rooted as a tree.
Now, Willow, I weep.
                              --Pam Ewing

LONELY

When you are lonely, where can you go?
When your spirits are down and you really
    feel low?
You walk in the park
    where a quiet breeze blows.
You're feeling lonely,
    but nobody knows.

You meet a nice person,
    You talk for a while.
You grin and you laugh,
    And you run and you smile.

You're happy now--
You've found a friend.

                                        --Lee Kellems

I WANT TO FLY

I want to fly
Like a bird
Like a plane that can sing
Like an eagle that soars
I want to fly--
I want to fly.

Sweet Kingdom of the Wind,
I don't know just how;
My life's just begun
But some way, Wind,
But some day, Wind,
I want to fly.

Dear sweet Wind,
I don't know how,
But some way
Take me into flight,
To the Kingdom of the Wind.

I want to fly
To fly over mountain and plain
To come back again
And proclaim my great feat
I want to fly.
With every bone in my body;
I want to fly--I want to fly--
I want to fly ... I want to ...

                                        --Pam Ewing

MY WISH

I wish I were a bird
Flying very high.
I would fly over hills
That were waiting just for me.
At night I would keep warm
In my castle tree home.

                                        --Bruce Kell

SCOUT MOTHER'S LAMENT

One day I was sleeping so peaceful and nice,
When I heard a loud clatter--I thought
    It was mice.
Then it hit me--I knew right then--
Trouble was back to begin again.
The kids were home from camp at last.
I'd have to unpack and unpack--
    What a task!
They're hungry, I'll bet.
Well, I'll fix them some lunch by the T. V. set.
    Peanut butter and ham and bread--
    No, that's wrong--they'll want lunch meat
        instead.
Ye gads! Here they come!

Their clothes need washing, they're dirty
    All over,
And they don't smell exactly like clover.

But these are my kids
And I love them all,
Big and skinny,
Short and tall.

I love them home from camp.
                              --Lee Kellems

A NICE PLACE TO BE

My house is a nice place to be.
My pal and I sit in a turret,
A turret full of books
As far as your eyes can see
All the way from A to Z
For my imaginary friend and me.
                        --Rebecca Pfettscher

At this time of developing a wider vocabulary and
discovering meanings and subtleties, there is a growing
interest in using a dictionary and a good thesaurus. Each
new word learned is an excitement and delight in itself.

When someone said, "I saw a bunch of cows," another
child suggested finding a better word for "bunch," a search
began which resulted in the satisfaction of using the right

word in the right place.   Some of the rewarding findings
were

A herd of cows	A bevy of quails
A flock of sheep	An exultation of larks
A colony of bees	A gaggle of geese
A drift of pigs	A muster of peacocks
A brood of hens	A raft of ducks
A flight of doves	A watch of nightingales
A school of fish	A whiteness of swan
A pride of lions	A cowardice of curs
A kindle of kittens	A smack of jellyfish
A trip of goats	A congregation of rooks
A pod of whales	A siege of herons
A train of camels	A charm of goldfinches

David Pannkuk used "kindle" of kittens effectively in his
cinquain in Chapter 2 (page 23).

As ability in writing increases, encourage the habit
of keeping a notebook to record new words, fleeting percep-
tions, sensory impressions, lines and phrases that come
unexpectedly and sing in the head. (From single lines, a
poem often grows.) A notebook is also handy for keeping
favorite poems, always giving the poet's name and where
the poem was found so it can be located readily if desired.

The basic value of any adventure in poetry with children is that the poetic vision apparently born in all babies
has been recognized and nurtured. Every child involved in
poetry appreciation and participation has been offered a
touchstone for testing life as truly as the ancients used a
smooth, fine-grained stone to test the purity of gold and
silver.   Poetry is a touchstone to be treasured for life.

Chapter 6

THROW ANOTHER LOG ON THE FIRE

The bright flame of poetry fluctuates in general appeal
over various periods of history and in various parts of the
world. During the 1960's there was a question of whether
or not poetry would ever again flourish among us. The
answer was "No" from the prophets of doom who predicted
that as our age becomes more and more technical and mech-
anized, the symbolic forms of expression would steadily
decline and become of interest only to a small esoteric seg-
ment of society and lose its appeal to the masses.

This chilling forecast must have prompted Helen
Bevington, poet, teacher and author of many books, to write:

> I wish I could read a book, not to be written in
> my lifetime, The History of Poetry in the Atomic
> Age, or The Rise and Fall of Poetry--a book that
> will reveal whether poetry managed to survive and
> last out the century, or went straight to the dogs.
> It will say how the poetic revolution came out, the
> counter-revolution, and the counter-counter revolu-
> tion, who won or lost the war of words.... In
> a century of wars, poetry has fought its bloody
> own in the thick of battle. At this dismal moment,
> the conqueror seems to be prose. [From When
> Found, Make a Verse Of]*

*Reprinted by permission of the author.

The spark of poetry need never be extinguished entirely. When recognized at home, at school, in libraries, and in the community there is ample fuel to strengthen life-giving powers of poetry as a source of joy, a means of communication, and a way of discovering truth that nothing else can replace.

Poets-in-residence appear on the faculty of colleges and universities; poetry workshops and seminars abound; poetry readings by individuals and by groups thrive with increasing interest. The scene is not limited to places of higher learning, but may be found in coffee houses, community centers, and even in many parks.

Poetry contests engender enthusiastic response on all age levels. The Evansville Arts and Education Council sponsors an annual poetry contest for children in grades one through twelve. The first year of the contest, several hundred children submitted original poems and a Poetry Festival was held in connection with The Ohio River Arts Festival. The winning poems were read aloud by members of the judging committee at a special program for relatives and friends in the formal lounge at the University of Evansville. A professional mime prepared ahead an interpretation of each poem and performed during the readings to the delight of the children and guests.

Following this first event, interest grew to include surrounding communities, and the number of entries more than tripled during the ensuing years. Miming, along with a ballet group from The Institute for the Fine and Performing Arts, continues to be part of the recognition ceremony which is now held in the university theater auditorium to accomodate the increased audience. The program was also aired on a local TV station. Each year an attractive booklet of the winning poems is prepared with the combined efforts of community organizations and individuals.

Another program, "Artists-In-Schools," is sponsored by the Indiana Arts Commission, partially funded by the National Endowment for the Arts. The program provides employment of professional artists in elementary and secondary schools (at their request) for the purposes of enhancing the students' aesthetic perception and ability to express themselves through various art forms including poetry and other creative writing, dance, craft and folk art, composing, filmmaking, theater, and visual arts. Artists may be in residence for a nine-month period, a four-month, a ten-week or shorter term.

All over the country, similar projects are being established to bring the arts and curriculum education together. In her book To Defend a Form, Ardis Kimzy presents a comprehensive study of the administration and teaching techniques for the North Carolina program, "Poetry-in-the-Schools."

The presence of a visiting poet is an exciting and inspiring highlight for aspiring poets. Eve Merriam, poet, author, and consultant for creative writing by children, was a guest of The Evansville Public Library and met with the poetry group, relatives and friends. When she was introduced as a poet who writes wonderful books for children, Thomas jumped to his feet and announced, "I am a poet, too." His pride and self-confidence created a warm, relaxed atmosphere and brought a smile of understanding from Miss Merriam. Writing poetry was immediately removed from a remote, esoteric pursuit limited to a select few to a rewarding adventure for everyone.

There are, no doubt, practicing poets in every community who would gladly accept an invitation to meet with the children for a reading session and the children welcome their company. Pauline Fehn, a friend of mine who is not only a poet but an accomplished flutist, is very generous in sharing her talents with children's groups.

Music, in itself, is a natural and felicitious complement to poetry. A young man, Michael Goebel, an employee of The Evansville Public Library, gave us a treat of folk songs and songs he had written himself, accompanied by his guitar. Children become aware that their own verses may be set to music or that they can write lyrics for music already composed. (This was accomplished by the poetry class in the University of Evansville Fine Arts Program-- see pages 41-42).

On another occasion, folk songs were presented with dulcimer music by William Cox, string instrument specialist for the Evansville Vanderburgh School Corporation and hand-crafter of fine dulcimers.

If possible, invite a mime to interpret the children's poems through body movements after studying the contribu-

tions.   Michael Boengh, teacher and professional mime in
our community, is very adept at his art.   In traditional
black garb and white-face make-up, Michael weaves magic
for his viewers.   To see one's own poems come alive through
action is a fascinating experience.

A mime may often be found in a high school or college,
or through an Arts and Education Council, or any group
dedicated to the performing arts.   Where none can be found,
try to encourage the formation of a mime troop in your own
locality.   A good book for practical suggestions is The Mime
Book by Claude Kepnis.

With very little direction, the children themselves
become interested in miming poems of action.   Beginning
very simply with Mother Goose rhymes, children can very
easily move into acting out more challenging categories including their own.

Another invitational program is one prepared by the
children, consisting of their own poems selected to present
to relatives and other interested guests.   Choral reading is
also appropriate at this time.   Poetry has been spoken in
unison since ancient times, notably in Greek drama and
among American Indians.   In the spirit of co-operation, children of all ages, even the youngest chanting finger-plays
together, find great satisfaction in choral reading, particularly
the timid child who is reluctant to "solo" and who overcomes
self-consciousness by joining with others.   Excellent explanations of choral speaking and verse choirs are to be found in
Children and Books by May Hill Arbuthnot and Let's Enjoy
Poetry by Rosalind Hughes.

To prepare for choral speaking, read the chosen
poem aloud several times and help the children find the
rhythm.   There should be no sing-song tones nor careless
enunciation of the words.   The children may want to discuss
the meaning of the poem and discover who is speaking--
whether there is one voice, two voices or more.   When
there is one voice, the children speak in unison as in a
psalm from the Bible or in a poem like "Spring Song" by
William Blake.

SPRING SONG

Spring is coming, spring is coming,
    Birdies, build your nest;

Weave together straw and feather,
Doing each your best.

Spring is coming, spring is coming,
Flowers are coming too,
Pansies, lilies, daffodillies
Now are coming through.

Spring is coming, spring is coming,
All around is fair,
Shimmer and quiver on the river,
Joy is everywhere.

When there are two voices in dialogue, the group is divided into two sections; first one group speaks, then the second. Simple verses are good for beginners or for warming up.

BELL HORSES

1. Bell Horses, bell horses,
What time of day?

2. One o'clock, two o'clock,
Three and away.

PUSSY CAT

"Pussy-cat, pussy-cat,
Where have you been?"
"I've been to London
To visit the Queen."
"Pussy-cat, pussy-cat,
What did you there?"
"I frightened a little mouse
Under her chair."
                    --Mother Goose

BOW, WOW, WOW

Bow, wow, wow!
Whose dog art thou?
Little Tommy Tucker's dog.
Bow, wow, wow!
                    --Mother Goose

OLD WOMAN

"Old woman, old woman, shall
    we go a-hearing?"
"Speak a little louder, sir,
    I am very thick of hearing."
"Old woman, old woman, shall
    we go a-gleaning??"
"Speak a little louder, Sir,
    I cannot tell your meaning."
"Old woman, old woman, shall
    we go a-walking?"
"Speak a little louder, Sir,
    or what's the use of talking?"
"Old woman, old woman, shall
    I kiss you dearly?"
"Thank you, kind Sir,
    I hear you very clearly."

                              --Mother Goose

Poems with a refrain lend themselves well to a choral reading of two sections, one section (or one individual) speaking alternately with a chorus of voices repeating the refrain. A short example is one from Mother Goose:

THE BIG CLOCK

1.   Slowly ticks the big clock;

2.   Tick-tock, tick-tock!

1.   But Cuckoo clock ticks double quick;

2.   Tick-a-tock-a, Tick-a-tock-a.
     Tick-a-tock-a, tick!

A longer one from Mother Goose with chorus is:

A FARMER WENT TROTTING

Solo: A farmer went trotting upon his gray mare,
Chorus: Bumpety, bumpety, bump!
Solo: With his daughter behind him so rosy and fair,
Chorus: Lumpety, lumpety, lump!

S: A raven cried croak! and they all tumbled down,
C: Bumpety, bumpety, bump!

S: The mare broke her knees, and the farmer his crown,
C̲:   Lumpety, lumpety, lump!

S: The mischievous raven flew laughing away,
C̲:   Bumpety, bumpety, bump!
S̲:   And vowed he would serve them the same the next day,
C̲:   Lumpety, lumpety, lump!

On a larger scale, a program of poetry, "From Mother Goose To Shakespeare," was presented in an elementary school auditorium with a background reader as children acted out selections, ranging through traditional and modern favorites.

Poetry groups meeting in libraries have access not only to books but often find other valuable approaches to poetry appreciation. Shadow boxes and varied exhibits provide visual beacons for stretching the imagination and for leading to wide avenues of thought.

Shown in the Evansville library system, provocative portrayals include scenes from Alice in Wonderland, Raggedy Ann, Peter Rabbit and classics by Beatrix Potter; costumes and customs of foreign countries, such as Mexico and Japan; African art; games in Britain; units on space, oceanography, inventions, transportation, birds and nests, nature trails, shells, dolls, mythology, science fiction, and the list goes on.

Listening to records and cassettes of poetry readings is an enriching addition to poetry appreciation. This can be done at a regular meeting of the group or enjoyed individually at any time in libraries which have an audio system with headphones where a child may make a request and plug in for poetry while seated at a listening carrel.

In addition to activities indoors, we occasionally take ourselves outside. A leisurely walk is often inspiring. Perhaps there is a grassy plot just outside the door, perhaps there are a few trees, perhaps there is a busy thoroughfare, lively with human interest, inviting observation and awareness. One of our libraries has a small grassy area bordered by bright flower beds, inviting our attention. Another is adjoined by a tree-filled city park, lively with bird song and scampering squirrels.

In the university program, a walk around the campus

gave first-hand experience to our senses. We heard the
sound of bells ringing; we heard voices near and far; we
listened to birds singing and to bird calls. We saw squirrels at play and observed the shapes of trees and their individual leaves. We felt the velvety backs of certain leaves
and the resiliency of the grass, then picked a wide green
blade to whistle through or picked a blade of sour grass to
taste. We caught the sweet smell of flowering shrubs and
faint aromas, usually passed unnoticed.

At times we go farther afield. In a shopping center
near the library, an exhibit of driftwood art offered an inspiring trip. After viewing the fantasy of driftwood shapes,
the children gave voice to the imagination of the artist; the
resulting poems are included in Chapter 4 (pages 50-51).

We were invited to participate in the Rain Tree Arts
and Crafts Festival in nearby New Harmony, Indiana, held
when the raintrees bloom golden. A visual presentation
seemed most appropriate, prompting the children to print
copies of their poems which were then mounted on large
sheets of colored paper or other material of their choice.
Some were on flowered cloth or vivid print, some on colored
felt and some on burlap--all to be hung by clothespins on a
line stretched between two trees in the park. Since the art
and crafts at the festival were for sale, a printed sign announced "10¢ a Poem." The clothesline sale proved popular
with the visitors and with the children. No one became
wealthy, but the experience was rich and rewarding.

Poetry study groups should be prepared to reach into
the community and contribute significantly in a variety of
ways. As part of the summer Ohio River Arts and Crafts
Festival in Evansville, exhibitors line Main Street along the
walkway for the viewing pleasure of large crowds. Poetry
by children has been added to the other creative displays.
Poems can be seen to best advantage by being tied or fas-
tened with chothespins to the branches of a tree dubbed the
"Poet Tree," A simulated tree can be made from heavy
cardboard or plywood if a live tree is not growing in the
chosen location. Branches from a real tree can be brought
in for the occasion.

The concept of the "Poet Tree" is also used by the
University poetry class on the last day of the session when
visitors are invited to a picnic and a viewing of the children's work. The trunk of a large live oak is circled with

colored twine to hold poems which can easily be read by
the guests.

Each community and each situation will offer its individual opportunity for participation according to its own
occasions and celebrations.

Further valuable suggestions may be found in books
and articles which have been written in the past few years
plus an increasing number of contemporary publications
giving one person's experience in sharing poetry with children. A sampling of such material is listed in the Section
Suggestions for Further Reading. The variety of approaches
should not be intimidating nor confusing, but should encourage
selectivity and further reading.

Teaching creative writing is at its best a creative en-
deavor and should never be reduced to a method or formula.
Nor should anyone become self-conscious or uneasy about
choosing a "best way" since there could never be found just
one way for all situations. Investigating many sources will
help you discover a plan you like and feel comfortable pur-
suing. Some are best used with one child, some with a
group; some with the younger age and some with older children. By trying out various suggestions, you will be able
to discover those that the children react to with the most
enthusiasm and those that produce the best results.

Aileen Fisher, who is praised as a true poet--no
mere light versifier--in a review of her book Out in the
Dark and Daylight (Harper & Row, 1980), is concerned about
bringing children and poetry together. She emphasizes that
poetry should "say something" and that more poetry should
be written because of the role of science in today's world.
She feels that there is even greater need to help the child
understand his or her environment through poetry.

A child's world would be incomplete without the magic
of poetry as a source of joy as well as a response to experience expressed in a significant way. Sharing poetry with
and by children brings an added dimension to life for them
and for us. When we see the brightening faces of young
people as they grasp the beautiful meaning or humor of a
poem, there is a realization that something important has
happened and that all of us are born poets with a need to
keep the spark alive.

Chapter 7

ADD COLOR TO THE FLAMES

There is not likely to be an end to discovering subject matter for writing poems, jingles, chants, and verses, nor a dearth of forms in which to write them. In addition to time-honored poetic inventions, interesting new ones continue to appear.

Many adults presenting poetry to children know only the old favorites of a long-ago childhood. Bogged down by lack of time or lack of interest, or because they feel safer sticking with traditional poetry and limited forms, they are missing the wonderful opportunity of widening their own horizons.

Dipping into general anthologies and specific collections, as well as books of poetry by a single author, offers the best way to become acquainted with forms not widely experienced and with poetry appropriate to contemporary interests and to the language of today's children.

For a change of pace and a pleasant diversion, children enjoy experimenting with verse forms that differ in part from the traditional and familiar. These "off-the-beaten-path" forms are more like a game or a puzzle and present a challenge to the writer's inventiveness and imagination.

Concrete Poetry

This form is also called "Picture Poetry" since the

poem's message springs not only from the meaning of the
words but also from the arrangement of the words and letters which make a picture.   The poem becomes visual by
taking a shape appropriate to the subject matter.   Advertisers
value this form since it immediately catches the eye of the
reader as shown in the following examples.

```
                    IT USED TO BE
                    THE GUY WHO
                     WORE THE
                        TIE
                      BUT NOW
                    GIRLS BUY
                    TIES,    NOT
                   JUST FOR GUYS
                  FOR   THEMSELVES
                 THEY BUY TIES WITH
                POLKA DOTS,TIES WITH
                SPOTS, TIES WITH POP ART
                TIES WITH WORDS ON
                THEM, TIES WITH A
                 BIRTHSTONE, TIES
                  WITH PICTURES,
                   STRIPES AND
                     CHECKS.
                      TIES.
```

                              - Lisa Klinger

```
                    I
                  wish
                I were a
               kite on high
        I could fly up to the sky
         Up to the blue sky
          High as a cloud
          I wish I were
              A kite
               High
                 Up
                 Up
                 Up
                 Up
                  +
                   +
                    +
                     +
                      +
                       +
```

                    Thomas Goodloe

Rain

```
p   i   t   t   e   r          p   a   t   t   e   r
i   i                          a   a
t       t                      t       t
t           t                  t           t
e               e              e               e
r   a   i   n       r          r   a   i   n       r
```

                                          - Robert Fleming

    Lewis Carroll has an excellent example of concrete verse in Chapter III ("A Circus Race and a Long Tale,") of Alice's Adventures in Wonderland. The poem is written in the shape of a mouse's tail as you can see on page 91.

The Clerihew

    Edmund Clerihew Bentley thought up a form based on names and then gave it his own middle name. A clerihew is a simple form--a quatrain in which the first two lines rhyme and the last two lines have another rhyme.

> Edmund Clerihew Bentley
> Loved words most intently.
> And for something to do
> He thought up the clerihew.

The subject may be one's own name, friends, family, or famous names from history, politics, sports, TV or movie personalities.

Dada Poetry

    This form is fun to try and requires a little action and a few materials. To compose dada poetry, the children should have on hand old newspapers, paper bags, scissors and paste. A paragraph is clipped from the newspaper and the words cut apart. These are put into the paper bag, which the children shake up with great fervor, then draw out the words one by one and arrange them in the order drawn. (It is permissible to throw away one occasionally if "the" or "and" appears twice in a row. It is also fair to shift the words about when necessary for a better line.)

    Dadaism got its start in Zurich, Switzerland during

```
                   Mouse's Tail

            Fury said to
             a mouse, That
                     he met
                      in the
                      house,
                      'Let us
                  both go
                  to law:
                I will
              prosecute
            you.
              Come, I'll
                take no
                    denial;
                      We must
                          have a
                              trial;
                                  For
                              really
                        this
                          morning
                              I've
                          nothing
                      to do.'
                  Said the
                mouse to
               the cur,
               'Such a
                   trial,
                 dear sir,
             With no
           jury or
          judge,
            would be
              wasting
                our breath.'
                    'I'll be
                    judge,
                I'll be
          jury,'
         Said
             cunning
               old Fury;
                 'I'll try
                    the whole
                          cause,
                        and
                      condemn
                        you
                          to
                            death.'

                           -Lewis Carroll
```

World War I with a group of rebellious young artists who
thought the world was going nowhere.   The movement in art
and literature rejected the standards and values of society
by proposing unrestrained expression in behavior and artistic form.   Picasso stuck odd bits of newspapers on gag
paintings in a wonderful display of color.   Interesting dada
poems can be achieved by children in an absorbing session.
If a child complains that no "good" words are coming out,
suggest dumping that bagful and starting over with another
clipping.   Even ads can be satisfying.

FASHION NOTE

    Short solid checks,
    Backward sizes,
    Solids with solids,
    Tennis in reds,
    Dresses 6x in blue A-line.
    Bloomers, stripes and prints.
    Elastic matching shift tops.
                                    --Cheryl Martin

CHRISTMAS IN MID-AFTERNOON

Christmas is appropriate with family,
    Simple cooperation,
        Yourself having breakfast on a simple tray
        Right gala breakfast.
Sit on the hour
    Happy as Mother,
        You'll like the prospect,
            One served on the house,
                Breakfast is something merry
                Served in the alley.
                                    --Jeanne Roller

IT'S OH!   FOR JUMPING

Hang any hour in window.
It rains for spattered toads,
A traverse kind.
Perhaps he can beg someone.

When will frog find a number for jumping?
And what exposures of time identify?
                                    --Ann Carpenter

LIGHT-HEARTED DOG SCHOOL

Fitted mincing kingdom about attraction,
Owners and sturdy, silly, little is pungently.
Heart, intelligent, talking, sporting poodle.
Not from water wrathful the animals.
Mincer has and loves that second--even all.
Lighthearted love, walk, wave off ...
School for dogs.
                              --Bruce and Melanie Kell

Dada poetry provides a bagful of images and a roomful of
laughter.

The Diamante

This poetry pattern was invented by Iris M. Tiedt
who was searching for varied ways to stimulate the writing
of poetry by young writers. The diamante (dee-ah-mahn'-
tay) follows this diamond shaped pattern and changes in
meaning from top to bottom.

Love--

Beautiful, happy

Sharing, confiding, touching

Friends,   you,   me,   world,   universe

Teaching, leading, growing

Lonely, furious

Hate.
                              --Group poem

The result of this experiment is a seven-line contrast
poem changing in meaning from beginning to end by following the order of words and lines.

1. Choose a noun
2. Two adjectives describing the noun
3. Three participles (words ending in ing or ed)
    pertaining to the noun
4. Four nouns related to the subject
5. Three participles indicating change or develop-
    ment of the subject noun
6. Two adjectives of complete change
7. A noun that is the opposite of the subject noun

This procedure is too difficult for the younger children and
some of the older ones, but may be introduced as a group
poem to help get acquainted with the form.   It is interesting
to use for poems on exhibit with colorful backgrounds or art
work.

Occasionally a child will run across a humorous
epitaph such as "Epitaph on a Dormouse, which some Children were to bury"

> In paper case,
> Hard by this place,
> Dead a poor dormouse lies:
> And soon or late,
> Summoned by fate,
> Each prince, each monarch dies.
>
> Ye sons of verse,
> While I rehearse,
> Attend instructive rhyme;
> No sins had Dor
> To answer for,
> Repent of yours in time.

--Anonymous

An epitaph by definition is a short statement in memory of
a dead person, usually put on his gravestone.   There are
many humorous ones in rhyme which older children like to
use as models.

> Here lies old Tom Tuckertu,
> Noted for his whopping lies.
> Now with nothing else to do,
> He simply lies, and lies and lies.

Found Poetry

This form is just what the name implies.   Passages
of prose that sound like poetry can be found in books by
writers whose prose passages are filled with rhythm and
imagery.   Everyone has probably thought at some time,
"That sounds like poetry" when reading A. A. Milne, Beatrix Potter, Kenneth Grahame, E. B. White and all who
use language in a beautiful style.   Students in adult literature classes have been encouraged to find passages in Look
Homeward, Angel by Thomas Wolfe and to arrange the lines in
poetic form.

    In addition to books and stories in magazines, in-
triguing verse material can be found in some of the most
unlikely places: newspapers, advertisements, signs on city
streets and along country highways, directions in buildings,
and even in scientific reports.   The distinguished poet Mari-
anne Moore frequently used lines from newspaper ads and
accounts of sports events in her adult poetry.   We can take
the advice of Helen Bevington from the title of one of her
books, When Found, Make a Verse Of.

    At an after-school poetry meeting in the basement of
our downtown Central Library, a little girl noticed a sign
in the hall as she was coming in for our meeting: "Fallout
Shelter."   As we gathered cozily at a large round table,
Karen made an observation which she wrote as a found poem.

FALLOUT SHELTER

If the atom bomb comes,
I hope we're all here together
in the library.
It would be more fun than anyplace else.
And we'd have all these books
to save for posterity.
And we'd have the coke machine in the hall.

Another found poem from a sign was written by Kari Points;
see "Insurance" on page 54.   Terse verse is often found on
signs: "Go/Slow," "Root Beer/Sold Here."   The TV com-
mercial of a national hamburger chain has good possibilities
as a springboard: "Our hamburgers are poetry on a bun."

    A charming cookbook, The Wild Flavor, by my friend
Marilyn Kluger, contains passages of delectable "found
poetry" along with delectable recipes for wild foods found
in field and forest.   For example:

The wild strawberry field invites, entices, wel-
    comes,
With bees at greenish-white heads of clover
And butterflies hovering over
Heavy-scented milkweed blossoms.
We settle down in a drift of white field daisies
And fill our baskets with bouquets of scarlet straw-
    berries.

Poetic lines can be found throughout How the Heather

<u>Looks</u> by Joan Bodger, a family's literary tour of England
<u>with</u> two-and-a-half year old Lucy and Ian, almost nine.
Notable are these:

> Lucy was soggy from sleep
> And I was soggy from Lucy.

>   .   .   .

> "That be jolly hot, that!" she said
> And wrapped the loaf in a piece of newspaper
> For me to carry.
> Oh, how good it smelled!
> And it was better than a fur tippet
> To carry against the chill.

There are many verse forms originating in foreign
countries, but one which is known in countries around the
world is the Grook (rhymes with "kook"). A Danish poet-
scientist named Piet Hein began writing defiant verses when
the German troops were occupying Denmark during World
War II. They contained hidden messages which the Germans
did not understand, but the Danes did. They became so
popular that Piet Hein kept on writing more and more short,
humorous, and meaningful comments about life. The Grook
(spelled <u>gruk</u> in Denmark) has no set form. Most of them
rhyme, but do not always have the same form. Many children write Grooks without knowing the name, but it's more
fun if they do.

Examples of children's poems that fulfill the specified
qualities of being short, humorous, and expressing a meaningful comment about life: "Busy People" by Becky Underwood on page 73 and the following by Frank Kanowsky:

QUESTION

> He may be a king,
> He may wear a ring.
> He may try to sing,

> He may have some money,
> He may not be a dummy,
> He may play gin rummy,

> But may still be a king.

Another experimental form originating in Japan is the

haiku which has been discussed on page 21 with rules for
writing this form and examples.   It seems strange that a
survey (page 101) of children's preferences in poetry puts
haiku low on the list.   Perhaps it is because they are introduced to those beyond their comprehension and experience.
Interest and appreciation are more likely to be created by
reading haiku which contain humor and relationship to everyday life.   Enjoyable haiku for children can be found in Cherry-
Blossoms, translations of poems by Basho, Buson, Issa,
Shiki and other old masters.   What child could resist this
one:

> O you snub-nosed doll!
> Maybe your mother didn't
> Pinch and pull enough.
>
> --Buson

While the haiku almost always has a keyword, some
of these do not, but all the poems are arranged by seasons.
Children enjoy Cricket Songs by Harry Behn as an introduction to a three-line, unrhymed poem and are eager to try
their own.   The mother of a boy in the library poetry group
phoned me one night to ask, "What is this haiku Josh is
talking about?"   I explained the rules and some time later
she called again to tell me how much the entire family enjoyed this writing project together.

I am reminded of a newspaper article I read some
time ago about poetry ceremonial readings in Japan.   The
Emperor has held an annual contest open to everyone--
teachers, farmers, housewives, and bureaucrats--even the
emperor and empress themselves compete.   The poems submitted must be in the tanka form which is related to haiku,
having five lines of 5-7-5-7-7 syllables.   A tanka in English
may consist of five short lines without an exact number of
syllables.   Each year a subject is given.   One year the
subject was fish and my library group tried one of their
own:

TANKA

> Golden shafts of light
> Dart about my goldfish bowl,
> Playing hide-and-seek,
> In and out through swaying green
> Or out of sight behind grey rocks.

In Japan, the poems must be written with a calligraphy brush

on a special kind of paper. The fifteen best poems out of
thousands received one year were chanted in an ancient style
by seven readers--sometimes in a chorus, sometimes as a
solo voice as the emperor and empress sat before a golden
screen.

Haiku written by children are not always perfect in
form and content but give the writers a sense of accomplish-
ment, the experience of following a discipline, and free many
from the notion that all poetry must rhyme.

Parody appeals to children of all ages according to
the understanding of the poem being parodied. By definition,
a parody in verse is a humorous imitation of another verse
which is not necessarily humorous itself. The parody follows
the form of the original changing its sense to nonsense.
Young children (and even older ones) find parodies of Mother
Goose verses hilarious, and like to make up their own.

> Hickory, dickory, dock!
> The mouse ran up the clock;
> The clock struck one,
> The doctor went out to lunch.

> There was an old woman who lived in a shoe,
> She had so many children she didn't know what to do.
> She gave them some broth without any bread,
> And took them all out to the zoo.

Older children who might be familiar with Shakespeare's
line "To be or not to be ... " would appreciate the parody
of that line: "To sneeze or not to sneeze, that is the question,": or Mark Antony's famous words from Julius Caesar:

> "Friends, Romans, countrymen, lend me your ears;
> I will give them back next Saturday."

This line from a parody of Gray's Elegy by Gelett Burgess
and Burges Johnson--"The short and simple flannels of the
poor"--changes only one word: "annals" to "flannels." A
good book to use with the children when introducing parody
is Speak Roughly to Your Little Boy: A Collection of Parodies and Burlesques Together with Original Poems Chosen
and Annotated for Young People (Harcourt, 1971), edited by
Myra Cohn Livingston.

There is such a vast store of poetic forms and poetic

terms that there is almost no end.   Two excellent resource
books are The Princeton Encyclopedia of Poetry and Poetics,
edited by Alex Preminger (Princeton University Press, N. J.,
1974) and Poetry Handbook; A Dictionary of Terms by Babette
Deutsch (Funk and Wagnalls, 1969).   How far you choose to
pursue the subject of poetry for your own appreciation and
enlightenment, and whether or not you use the more sophisticated and unfamiliar material with children must rest on
your own discretion.   The children themselves will usually
give you a clue as to how far their "reach should exceed
their grasp."   When a child asked, "What is a sonnet?"
I was glad to tell her and she was glad to know, but she
was not ready to try this complicated form.   Some day she
would be.   Children should not be given more information
than they can handle.   To paraphrase Shakespeare, their
reaction might be

> Some are born poets,
> Some achieve poetry,
> And some have poetry thrust upon them.

Chapter 8

WARMING TO THE GLOW

Reading poetry aloud to children, filling their ears with music and their minds with pictures, is still by far the best way to arouse their interest and to understand the techniques of writing poetry. With the rich variety of poems from the past as well as those being written in the present, it is possible to please the taste of almost everyone, even those who at first believe that all poetry can be lumped into one dish. A word of advice from Eve Merriam might whet a lagging appetite when she tells the reluctant reader how to eat a poem: "Don't be polite, bite in ... " (from her poem in It Doesn't Always Have to Rhyme). It is a surprise to discover that not all poetry is about love, truth and beauty.

I have found it useful to read from a book of poems on a particular subject. Interesting, original poems on color (see p. 60) have been inspired from using Hailstones and Halibut Bones by Mary O'Neill. Prayers from the Ark by Carmen Bernos De Gasztold, translated by Rumer Godden, offers models for children to write further animal prayers.

Collections of poetry written by children (such as Miracles collected by Richard Lewis and I Heard a Scream in the Street, poems by young people in the city selected by Nancy Larrick) bring confidence to children in their own abilities. For older children Rose, Where Did You Get That Red? by Kenneth Koch is an excellent combination of handbook, anthology, and instructor's guide containing selections by great poets of many periods of history along with poems by children.

Often a single poem by a famous poet can provide a
starting point for a group or an individual child. I have
mentioned "The Great Lover" by Rupert Brooke and "Barter" by
Sara Teasdale (p. 58) and "The End" by A. A. Milne (p. 61).
It is great fun to express "hates" instead of "loves" once in
a while. After reading "Horrible Things" by Roy Fuller--
found in Round About Six which begins "What is the horriblest
thing you've seen?"--children are quick to recount personal
observations in an original poem.

Famous poets are known to write on subjects which
children might not have considered proper or important
enough for poetry. The titles of may poems by the distinguished Chilean poet, Pablo Neruda, reveal this fact: "Ode
to My Socks," "Ode to the Watermelon," "Ode to Salt,"
"Ritual of My Legs," "A Lemon," "Artichoke," "To the Foot
from Its Child," "To Wash a Child," and others. Children
above the primary grades enjoy being introduced to "Ode to
My Socks" and "To the Foot from Its Child" and will be
excited by the possibilities of choosing simple, everyday
subjects.

In general, poetry is read and enjoyed on more than
one level. First is the surface level in which the literal
meaning is immediately perceptible; second is the interpreta-
tive or symbolic meaning, and third is the meaning one gets
from a personal response. The first and third are most
easily grasped by a child. There are fine poems written
for adults which should be shared with children. Blake's
"The Tyger" is found in anthologies for children and readily
accepted for its imagery and sound. "The Fish" by Elizabeth
Bishop is recommended for use with children for the same
reasons.

A national survey in grades four, five, and six was
presented in Children's Poetry Preferences, a paperback by
Ann Terry, which is one of a series of monographs sponsored by
the National Council of Teachers of English. Of 113 poems
selected for this study, representing traditional as well as
modern works, the two given the highest ratings by the children were "Mummy Slept Late and Daddy Fixed Breakfast"
by John Ciardi because it was funny and told a story and
"Eletelephony" by Laura E. Richards because of the made-
up funny words.

Others which were rated high were "Pickety Fence"
by David McCord because of the rhythm and sound of the

words, "We Real Cool" by Gwendolyn Brooks because it was
humorous and modern, "Adventures of Isabel" by Ogden Nash
because it was funny and told a story. Tongue-twisters were
popular because of the alliteration, and limericks because
they were funny and had a lot of rhyme.

    One of the most unpopular poems was the haiku be-
cause "It didn't have any rhyme," "It's too short," "It got
no story behind it," "I did not get nothing out of this poem."
(And yet, children seem to enjoy writing this form.) Imagery seemed to be a stumbling block for some children,
who dislike "The Red Wheelbarrow" by William Carlos Williams, "Silver" by Walter de la Mare, "Who Has Seen the
Wind?" by Christina Rossetti, and "April Rain Song" by Langston Hughes.

    Although there is a difference of preferences among
age groups and between boys and girls, poems are generally
disliked for these reasons: too short, not funny, did not
rhyme, no story, difficult to understand, and listening was
not enjoyable. On the other hand most children preferred
poems with a thread of humor, familiar experiences, narrative, interesting words, rhyme and rhythm.

A Sampling of Poems to
Kindle Other Poems

Oh, Such Foolishness!   Selected by William Cole, pictures
by Tomie de Paola.   Lippincott, 1978.
        Nonsense rhymes by well-known poets that will start
        the funny bone tickling and a poem brewing.

I'm Mad At You!   Selected by William Cole, illustrated by
George MacClain.   Collins, 1978.
        Humorous poems that give vent to anger and frustra-
        tion help children face their own negative feelings and
        to let off steam by expressing these pent-up emotions.

Munch.   Poems and pictures by Alexandra Wallner.   Crown,
1976.
        Humorous verse on the joys of eating and snacking
        that will encourage children to write about their own
        favorite foods.

Laughing Time by William Jay Smith.   Little, 1955.
        Funny, inventive poems to stir the imagination.

Of Quarks, Quasars, and Other Quirks--Quizzical Poems for
the Supersonic Age. Collected by Sara and John E. Brewton
and John Brewton Blackburn, illustrated by Quentin Blake.
Crowell, 1977.
>Full of timely, wacky poems that will certainly set
>off a new, modern train of thought.

Who would marry a mineral? Riddles, Runes & Love Tunes
by Lillian Morrison, decorations by Rita Floden Leyden.
Lothrop, 1978.
>Play with sound, letters, and form give pleasure as
>well as a spur toward the reader's creative efforts.

Poems Make Pictures--Pictures Make Poems by Giose Ri-
manelli and Paul Pimsleur, pictures by Ronni Solbert. Pan-
theon, 1972.
>Shows concrete poems written in appropriate shapes
>that children enjoy trying.

Moonfish and Owl Scratchings by George Mendoza, illustrated
by Peter Parnall. Grosset, 1971.
>Interesting pictures accompany short poems defining
>"a poem" in imaginative metaphors.

The Man in the Moon as He Sails the Sky and Other Moon
Verse. Collected and illustrated by Ann Schweninger. Dodd,
1979.
>The moon sails in many directions in verses by Mother
>Goose, jungles and poems by well-known poets, sure
>to stir the imagination of even the most reluctant.

The Dog Writes on the Window with His Nose, collected by
David Kherdian, pictures by Nonny Hogrogrian. Four Winds,
1977.
>Short poems by distinguished contemporary poets that
>young children will understand and enjoy although not
>all of the poems were written specifically for children.
>A good selection of poems that do not have to rhyme.

Come Play with Me by Margaret Hillert, illustrated in full
color by Kinuko Craft. Follett, 1975.
>A Follett Just Beginning-To-Read Book of Verse has
>simple rhymes for the youngest reader.

Round About Six, Poems for Today. Selected by Margaret G.
Rawlins, with illustrations by Denis Wrigley. Warne, 1973.
>Lively poems for younger children by well-known English
>and American poets with several written by children.

Round About Eight, Poems for Today. Selected by Geoffrey
Palmer and Noel Lloyd, illustrations by Denis Wrigley,
Warne, 1972.
>   The poets included range in age from round about
>   eight to round about eighty and cover all interests and
>   moods in poems from many countries and from all
>   times.

Dirty Dinkie and Other Poems. Collected by Theodore Roethke.
Doubleday, 1973.
>   This collection is especially interesting to children.

Good Morning to You, Valentine. Selected by Lee Bennett
Hopkins, illustrated by Tomie de Paola. Harcourt, 1976.

Easter Buds Are Springing. Selected by Lee Bennett Hopkins, illustrated by Tomie de Paola, Harcourt, 1979.
>   Both of these anthologies of holiday poems sparkle
>   with poems by well-known writers from William Shake-
>   speare to some Valentine poems that might have been
>   written by a child to scribble on a homemade card.
>   Previous books in this series center on Halloween,
>   Christmas, Independence Day, and Thanksgiving.

There are many other books on special topics:

The Bird Book. Compiled and edited by Richard Shaw.
Warne, 1974.
>   A choice collection of bird poems by famous poets
>   together with folk tales and legends.

Ghost Poems. Edited by Daisy Wallace, illustrated by Tomie
de Paola. Holiday House, 1979.
>   All kinds of ghosts in poems by all kinds of writers
>   tempt the children to write scary poems. Other titles
>   in this series include Giant Poems, illustrated by
>   Margot Tomes; Witch Poems, illustrated by Trina
>   Shart Hyman; Monster Poems, illustrated by Kay
>   Chorao. All of these subjects appeal to the interest
>   of children.

Strange Monsters of the Sea by Richard Armour, with pictures
by Paul Galdone. McGraw-Hill, 1979.
>   Another intriguing title with poems by the master of
>   light verse. The poems give facts about sea creatures
>   spiced with humor.

The Poetry of Horses. Collected by William Cole, illustrated
by Ruth Sanderson. Scribner's, 1979.
   One of many anthologies by Mr. Cole that concentrates
   on a single subject includes such fine present-day
   poets as May Swenson, Henry Taylor, Donald Hall
   and David Wagoner.

Mice Are Rather Nice. Selected by Vardine Moore, decora-
tions by Doug Jamison. Atheneum, 1981.
   Mouse poems from Mother Goose, famous childhood
   poets such as A. A. Milne, Aileen Fisher, Elizabeth
   Coatsworth, also from poets such as Edith Sitwell,
   William Stafford, and Robert Burns. For all ages.

My Mane Catches the Wind. Compiled by Lee Bennett Hopkins, drawings by Sam Savitt. Harcourt, 1979.
   More lively poems on a favorite subject.

I Am the Running Girl by Arnold Adoff, pictures by Ronald
Himler. Harper, 1979.
   Mr. Adoff's poems are good examples of the open
   form where the words flow down the page.

Crazy to be Alive in Such a Strange World. Selected by
Nancy Larrick, photographs by Alexander L. Crosby. M.
Evans, 1977.
   Poems about all kinds of people that will appeal to
   all ages but best understood by the older children.

The Covered Bridge House by Kaye Starbird, illustrated by
Jim Arnosky. Four Winds, 1979.
   Also about people--mostly oddballs--the poems are
   written with humor and insight.

Up the Down Elevator by Norma Farber, illustrated by Annie
Gusman. Addison-Wesley, 1979.
   Unusual characters board the elevator at each floor.
   Younger children recognizing the characters as well
   as numbers involved.

My Kind of Verse. Compiled by John Smith, illustrated by
Uli Shulevitz. Macmillan, 1968.
   Many important poets from the fifteenth century to the
   present are represented: Brecht, Cavafy, Coffin,
   Herrick, Lorca, Keats, Lindsay, Plath, Rilke, Shakespeare, Stevens, Yeats. The types of poetry include
   limerick, short narrative, nature poems, prayers, and
   odd character sketches.

A Flock of Words collected and annotated by David MacKay.
Harcourt, 1969.
>   Poems from many countries and centuries to be read
>   for pure enjoyment.

Reflections on a Gift of Watermelon Pickles (1966) and Some
Haystacks Don't Even Have Any Needles (1969).   Compiled by
Stephen Dunning, Edward Lueders, and Hugh Smith.   Scott,
Foresman.
>   Both of these collections have poems by well-known,
>   contemporary poets, and which will appeal to older
>   children.

Speak Roughly to Your Little Boy: A Collection of Parodies
and Burlesques Together with Original Poems Chosen and
Annotated by Young People.   Edited by Myra Cohn Livingston.
Harcourt, 1971.

The Phantom Ice Cream Man by X. J. Kennedy, Atheneum,
1979.
>   Witty and zany verse with the joy of rhythm and rhyme.

Go with the Poem.   Edited by Lillian Moore, McGraw, 1979.
>   Unrhymed poetry for older children by contemporary
>   American poets including Denise Levertov, William
>   Carlos Williams, William Stafford, and Lucille Clifton.

Out in the Dark and Daylight by Aileen Fisher, Harper, 1980.
>   Brief, gentle nature poems following the round of the
>   seasons, filled with awareness and insight.

Custard and Company.   Collected by Quentin Blake.   Little,
Brown, 1980.
>   Classic, humorous poems by Ogden Nash.

Morning, Noon and Nighttime, Too.   Collected by Lee Bennett
Hopkins, Harper, 1980.
>   Lively poems by William Jay Smith, Myra Cohn Liv-
>   ingston, Lillian Moore and other favorites follow chil-
>   dren through a school day from sun-up to sun-down.

Ed Emberly's ABC by Ed Emberly.   Little, Brown, 1978.
>   Springboard to the imagination with colorful, original
>   pictures.

Anno's Journey by Mitsumasa Anno.   William Collins, 1979.
>   Extends the imagination and creativity of all those who
>   travel with him.

They've Discovered a Head in the Box for the Bread.   Collected by John E. Brewton and Lorraine Blackburn.   Crowell,
        1978.   Limericks by famous authors; some with last
        lines to be finished by the reader.

Poems to Solve by May Swenson.   Charles Scribner's Sons, 1966.

A Sampling of Black Poetry

Brooks, Gwendolyn.   Bronzeville Boys and Girls.   E. M.
Hale, 1956.
        Appealing, original poems about children living in the
        inner city by the first black poet to receive a Pulitzer
        Prize for Poetry.

Giovanni, Nikki.   Spin a Soft Black Song: Poems for Children.
Hill and Wang, 1971.
        The poems in this book tell about universal, everyday
        experiences of children.

Randall, Dudley.   The Black Poets.   Bantam, 1979.
        Poems of interest for all grades.

                    For Upper Elementary Grades:

Adoff, Arnold.   Black Out Loud: Anthology of Modern Poems
by Black Americans.   Macmillan, 1970.
        Poems by such recognized names as Langston Hughes,
        LeRoi Jones, Margaret Walker as well as those of
        younger, less well-known artists.

_____.   I Am the Darker Brother.   Macmillan, 1968.
        An anthology of modern poems written by black Ameri-
        cans with brief biographies of the poets.

_____.   Where Wild Willie.   Harper, 1978.
        Verses of the free and happy play of a young child
        with a loving family in the background.   (Youngest
        children.)

Bontemps, Arna.   Golden Slippers: An Anthology of Negro
Poetry for Young Readers.   Harper, 1941.
        Selections from such familiar poets as Paul Laurence
        Dunbar, Claude McKay, Countee Cullen, and Langston
        Hughes along with traditional and spiritual ballads.

Hopkins, Lee Bennett, compiled by. Don't You Turn Back:
Poems by Langston Hughes.   Knopf, 1969.
    Forty-five poems by the poet laureate of black people.
    Introduction by Arna Bontemps.   (For children of all
    ages.)

Hughes, Langston.   New Negro Poets.   Indiana Press, 1964.
    Biographical notes on the poets are included.   (For
    more mature readers.)

Jordan, June.   Soulscript: Afro-American Poetry.   Doubleday, 1970.
    This collection contains the work of black master poets
    and features a section of "Hero Hymns and Heroines"
    including poetry about Malcom X, Harriet Tubman and
    Frederick Douglass.

_____.   Who Look at Me.   Crowell, 1969.
    A long, narrative poem with interesting paintings of
    American life.

Merriam, Eve.   I Am a Man: Ode to Martin Luther King,
Jr.   Doubleday, 1971.
    Although this is a picture book, the poem will appeal
    to older children.

Clifton, Lucille.   Some of the Days of Everett Anderson.   Holt,
1970.
_____.   Everett Anderson's Christmas Coming.   Holt, 1971.
_____.   Everett Anderson's Nine Month Long.   Holt, 1978.
    Beautiful, poetic stories of a little black boy's rela-
    tionships.

A Sampling of American Indian Poetry

Belting, Natalia.   Whirlwind Is a Ghost Dancing.   Dutton, 1974.

_____.   The Sun Is a Golden Earring.   Holt, 1962.
    Filled with poems of free-flowing imagery.

_____.   Our Fathers Had Powerful Songs.   Dutton, 1974.
    A collection of Indian song lore.

Bierhorst, John (edited by).   In the Trail of the Wind; American Indian Poems and Ritual Orations.   Farrar, 1971.
    Translations from over forty languages representing
    Indian cultures of North and South America.

Concha, Joseph L. Lonely Deer: Poems by a Pueblo Indian
Boy. Red Willow Society, 1969.
These poems are mostly about nature and the book
contains design-paintings by the seventeen-year-old
poet.

Jones, Hettie (compiled by). The Trees Stand Shining. Dial,
1971.
A picture book of songs with beautiful paintings by
Robert Andrew.

Wood, Nancy (collected by). Hollering Sun. Simon &
Schuster, 1972.
Poems, legends and sayings of the Taos Indians, with
excellent photographs by Myron Wood.

Lewis, Richard (edited by). I Breathe a New Song: Poems
of the Eskimo. Simon & Schuster, 1971.
An introduction to these poems by the anthropologist
Edmund Carpenter describes the people, their beliefs,
and their ways of forming poetry.

Hispanic

The Tamarindo Puppy by Charlotte Pomerantz. Greenwillow,
1980.
Childlike, lively poems in a blend of English and
Spanish.

Mother Goose on the Rio Grande by Frances Alexander.
Banks, 1944.
Although this is an old book, it may be useful with
Spanish-speaking children.

There's a Bull on My Balcony by Sesyle Joslin. Harcourt,
1966.
Helpful Spanish phrases.

Neruda and Vallejo. Selected by Robert Bly. Beacon Press,
1971.
Many of Neruda's poems are excellent to use with
children. This book contains English translations
along with the original Spanish.

¿ Que Sera? What Can It Be? Collected by Loretta Burke
Hubp. The John Day Company, 1970.

Traditional Spanish riddles with English translations
are all easy to read, and many are in rhyme.

Mother Goose in Spanish.   Translated by Alaistair Reid and
Anthony Kerrigan.   Thomas Y. Crowell Company, 1968.
Favorite Mother Goose rhymes translated into Spanish
have great charm, along with the beautiful pictures by
Barbara Cooney in this delightful book.

Suggested Recordings of Poetry Readings

An Anthology of Negro Poetry For Young People.   Arna Bontemps reads from his anthology Golden Slippers.   Folkways.

The Bat Poet.   By Randall Jarrell.   Read by the author.
Caedmon.

A Child's Garden of Verses.   By Robert Louis Stevenson.
Read by Judith Anderson.   Caedmon.

Discovering Rhythm and Rhyme in Poetry.   Read by Julie
Harris and David Wayne.   Caedmon.

Dream Keeper.   By Langston Hughes.   Read by the author.
Folkways.

A Golden Treasury of Poetry.   Prepared by Louis Untermeyer.
Read by Alexander Scourby.   Golden Records.

Gwendolyn Brooks Reading Her Poetry.   Caedmon.

How to Tell Corn Fairies and Other Rutabaga Stories.   By
Carl Sandburg.   Read by the author.   Caedmon.

The Hoosier Poet.   Poems by James Whitcomb Riley, read
by Robert Donley.   Listening Library, Inc.   Conn.

Let's Say Poetry Together.   Choral speaking for upper grades
by Carrie Rasmussen.   Activity Records, Ind.   Free-
port, N. Y.

The Nature of Poetry.   Lectures on poetry for older children
by Dr. Frank C. Baxter.   Spoken Arts.

Nonsense Verse--Carroll & Lear.   Read by Beatrice Lillie and
Cyril Ritchard.   Caedmon.

Old Possum's Book of "Practical Cats." By T. S. Eliot.
        Read by Robert Donat. Spoken Arts.

Pickety Fence and Other Poems. By David McCord. Read
        by the author. Pathways of Sound Inc.

Poems for the Very Young. Edited by Lucille Wood. Bow-
        man Records, Inc. Glendale, Calif.

Poet's Gold. Read by Helen Hayes, Thomas Massey and
        Thomas Mitchells. RCA Victor.

Poetry Parade. A two-record album edited by Nancy Larrick,
        produced by Weston Woods. Four top children's poets
        read their own words: David McCord, Harry Behn,
        Karla Kuskin, and Aileen Fisher.

        Dr. Larrick suggests that children need time along
the way to absorb and respond along the way when listening
to recordings since few will listen appreciatively without some
breaks for their own participation.

Chapter 9

EXTRA KINDLING

There will no doubt come dismal days when you feel at low ebb or the children are out of sorts with the weather, the world, or themselves. Do not be disheartened; this is the time to fall back on something light and just for fun, whether your ingenuity is tested at school, in the library poetry group, or at home. The following suggestions may be used individually or in a group.

Not everyone is inspired by the same idea at the same time, so it is helpful to have each suggestion on a separate file card, with a box of cards ready for the individual child to dip into and choose one that is appealing. Have another suggestion box ready from which you can choose. Some ideas from the two boxes may be interchangeable.

Group activities frequently pull dragging spirits out of the doldrums. A meter game will help children understand stressed and unstressed syllables. Begin with this observation: "Every word has some sort of meter with stressed and unstressed syllables, even your name. Let's try Ju-dy Meadows." Write it on the blackboard if you have one; if not, have the children write it on paper, marking the syllables. Then have each child give his own name with metrical emphasis. This is usually a surprising discovery, making the technique very personal. Next let them suggest words or take words from the dictionary noting the stresses.

Try a simile game by tossing out a random adjective or adverb, asking the children to make a comparison: "hot

as," "blue as," "quiet as," "angry as," "lonely as," "quickly
as," "stubborn like." Start with easy ones, but warn the
children not to use the first thing that pops into the mind.
Remind them that "hot as fire" and "cold as ice" are not
really comparisons and that "quiet as a mouse" is an old,
worn-out comparison. Phrases are permissible, even com-
mendable: "Quickly as a mouse frightened by a cat." These
comparisons might be written down and read aloud, or spoken
in turn.

A metaphor game may be played in a similar way.
Provocative nouns create pictures in the mind, so that imagery
becomes part of this practice: "The house was a crouching
animal peering into the darkness."

You can have a good time with personification by
choosing an inanimate object and giving it the power of speech.
"What do you think an automobile might say if it could talk?"
Give a few suggestions to prime the pump: "Good morning.
My tires are low," or "You forgot the keys again, Dummy."
(According to a recent newspaper article, the growing use
of technology makes this a real possibility.) Invite the children to select other objects to continue the game ... a tooth-
brush, perhaps, your bicycle, or your blue jeans.

The onomatopoeia game sounds difficult to children at
first because of its strange name, but it is actually the simplest one of all and probably the first figure of speech children
use. When children realize that they have been using this
poetic device since infancy, the response is immediate. They
quickly recognize that calling a cow a "moo-moo" is using
the sound that the cow makes; calling a dog a "bow-wow" and
a train a "choo-choo" were some of their first attempts at
verbalizing.

With the younger ones, begin with simple sounds: duck,
pig, horse, cow, rooster, frog, a hen, bee, pussycat, the
wind, etc. Then go on to more challenging concepts: "What
does the rain say?" You may get "pitter patter" or "splish
splash," or something you had never thought of yourself.
"What is the sound of popcorn popping, sudden stop of a car,
a hoe in the garden, a sneeze, a motorcycle taking off, a
bell or a drum?" Have a little fun by throwing in an occasional soundless image: snowflakes falling, a goldfish, a
rabbit, one hand clapping, turning over in a water bed. Soon
the word onomatopoeia loses its strangeness to children and
may become a means of expression in their own poetry.

Tongue twisters are popular for the sound of <u>alliteration.</u> One child might start with a word and the next <u>child</u> supply another word with the same beginning sound, and so on. Or each child may want to complete a tongue twister alone.

An excellent practice in <u>free association</u> is to give each child a list of words and suggest that they follow the word with a sound, smell, taste, feel, sight, or emotion which is personally related to that word preferably with a few details of the associated word: "pillow"--not "sleep" but "pillow"--"I like to stay all night at my grandmother's house because her pillows are filled with downy feathers and are very soft."

For capturing <u>vivid details</u>, suggest a scene to describe. For example take "A <u>Messy Room.</u>" "My socks were under the bed, a jelly sandwich on top of the spread, my jeans draped over the lamp, and my books were piled on the floor."

The natural rhythm that babies and very young children seem to have has been observed to falter and stumble later on. Playing the meter game helps to attune the ear to the singing quality of single words. Some teachers have also found that hearing poems of various rhythms and responding physically by marching, skipping, or dancing to the rhythm appeals to the play impulse and adds to the understanding of meter. In ancient times, the Greeks chanted poetry as they marched to the altar and back, noting how many footsteps were taken. So instead of always asking, "How many beats to the line?" we also say "How many feet to the measure?"

Rhythm is such an important part of poetry, body movements often accompany verse. Babies clap hands to "Pat-a-cake, pat-a-cake, baker's man!" or jounce on a friendly knee to the trotting rhythm of "Ride a cock horse to Banbury Cross."

With older children, jumping the rope is best enjoyed with jungles that resound to the timing of the turn of the rope. Counting out rhymes start games for choosing who is "it" or deciding who is "Out," or picking a leader.

In the kindergarten and primary grades, nursery rhymes suggest various movements for developing a sense of rhythm. For instance, <u>Pease porridge hot</u> has been enjoyed for generations as an intricate clapping game played with a partner. Other familiar rhymes to use are:

"Humpty Dumpty" for marching with high-stepping feet.
"I had a little pony" for galloping horses.
"Here we go round the mulberry bush" for gliding
    sideways.
"How do you like to go up in a swing" for swinging
    the arms from side to side, or pushing the arms
    forward and back (like pushing a rope swing).
"Diddle, diddle, dumpling, my son John!" for running
    on tip-toe.
"Jack be nimble" for jumping or hopping forward.
"Jack and Jill went up the hill" for skipping.
"Hickory Dickory Dock!" for running lightly.
"To Market, To Market." Can anybody do a jig?

These rhythms may be done in unison with one person
chanting the verses, or, if the group is large, half may chant
while the other half is in action.

An active game which younger children in particular
enjoy is a rhyme game played with a bouncing ball. Each
child in turn is given the ball and a word to rhyme: dog,
cat, hand, toe, yellow, leap, etc. The ball is bounced and
caught on each rhyming word and passed to the next child
when no more can be thought of. If a made-up word creeps
in now and then, it only adds to the fun.

Picture books can also be used as a springboard to
the imagination, particularly one like Ed Emberly's A B C,
(Little, Brown, 1978), which is filled with eye-dazzling pictures. The letter B, for example, shows a ladybug placing
blueberries along the lines that form the letter. A bear
wearing bifocals and watching the proceedings provides the
B word, also a nice alliteration.

Another delightful picture book is Anno's Journey by
Mitsumasa Anno. Without words, there is plenty of action
in each picture and wonderful detail strikes the fancy. These
books could be poured over by one child at a time, or two
could work together--finding funny scenes and engaging characters.

A quiet activity for all ages can be introduced by
making a picture collection of old greeting cards, picture
post cards, pictures from magazines, calendars, and colorful advertisements. Let each child choose one to write about;
some may want to bring a picture from home. This activity
not only provides subjects for poems, but also enlarges experience. There are children who have never seen a farm or

farm animal. Others may never have seen a skyscraper or
ocean liner. Few have been to a foreign country and none
have been to the moon. Pictures can give a visual dimension
to the meaning of poems and offer a vicarious experience.

It's safe to say that everybody loves a limerick.
Almost everyone tries to write one. Children will enjoy the
collection by John E. Brewton and Lorraine Blackburn, They've
Discovered a Head in the Box for the Bread and Other Laugh-
able Limericks. (Crowell), Edward Lear, the master of
limerick writing is here along with such notables as Eve Merriam, Oliver Hereford, Morris Bishop, William Jay Smith
and Walter de la Mare.

At the end of the book, there is a group of limericks
without a last line. To supply the missing lines is great
fun, and the children will, no doubt, want to go on making
up entire limericks of their own.

Poems to Solve by May Swenson is a selection of her
own poems for older children to make poetic discoveries.
They can play detective with the "riddle poems" in which the
subject is not mentioned in either the title or text. In "poems
to find," they must interpret allegory, metaphor, and fantasy
to learn what the poem is about. It is a challenge for older
children to write a poem to solve following Miss Swenson's
examples.

By the use of metaphor, the poet is able to suggest
the subject of a poem without mentioning it directly, but by
making comparisons in a hidden way. The metaphor creates
pictures in the mind until the subject becomes clear. When
Miss Swenson writes about an egg, she gives us a series of
pictures or images. One stanza begins "What's inside?
A sun?" This is far more interesting to the reader than
the obvious statement, "An egg is yellow inside."

A riddle game for younger children is called the pyramid.
This poem follows the form of a pyramid, each line giving
clues to the answer to the riddle. The first line is a noun,
the second line consists of two adjectives describing the noun,
the third line adds three verb forms, and the last line consists of a statement or question.

Pet

Brown, white

Biting, barking, running

Gives love and protection to its owner.

(Answer: A Dog)

Water

Wide, deep

Rolling, waving, splashing

Full of big ships, fish and submarines.

(Answer: Ocean)

Another riddle poem that is popular with children be-gins with "What in the world...."

What in the world
Carries a trunk,
Walks with a thump,
Looks like a pump,
Never does fuss,
Has a tusk,
Doesn't shave,
Never must?
(Elephant)

What in the world goes
Goo, goo, goo?
And when it awakes,
It plays with its toes
And maybe its nose?
(A baby)

One of the winners of a local contest told how she wrote her prize-winning poem. "A single line came to me, 'I stand in the valley.' It sounded like poetry so I went ahead, thinking about what I might see ... if you stand in a valley you would have to stand between something ... It was all imaginary, one line suggesting another":

I stand in the valley
Between our house and the hills,
Our peaceful red house,
The majestic black hills,
And the wind brings its own song
And echoes the hills--
Brings them to me,
Child of the hills.

Older children could practice this method of composing a poem. Two or three words come into your head, or maybe an entire line. You don't know from where nor why, but they

seem unusual or haunting like a part of a song. Write them
down and go on writing. Find words to go with the words
that have popped into your head. You might try to think of
words that rhyme with the last word of the line that is haunting you. The words you think of will suggest images. You
will begin to see the shape of the poem and hear its rhythm
and should be able to complete it.

Suggestions for Developing Word Appreciation

It is important to explore every opportunity to encourage words as excitement and delight in themselves since children change and grow in their use of words.

My friend Paul Darcy Boles, novelist and popular
workshop leader in numerous writers' conferences, finds
word games relaxing and helpful for workers in words. Mr.
Boles and his wife enjoy a rousing game of Probe on many
evenings when serious work is put aside temporarily. Other
word games can be kept on hand for children to enjoy and,
at the same time, enlarge their vocabularies. Popular boxed
word games on the market include Scrabble and Password.

Children of all ages love funny made-up words and
are adept at rolling them out in a verse:

OF ALL THE ANIMALS

Of all the animals there's the lion,
  Lion, splion, smidgy ion.
Of all the animals there's the mouse,
  Mouse, couse, smidgy ouse.
Of all the animals there's the kangaroo,
  Kangaroo, langeroo, smidgy angaroo.
Where do these animals come from?
  The Jungle!
Jungle, gungle, smidgy ungle.
                                        --Cheryl Martin

Another nonsense rhyme, playing with words is:

BILLY WILLY

Billy Willy is a dilly,
He took a pilly
And turned silly.

Silly dilly Billy Willy
Went up the hilly
And picked a lily.
Billy Willy gave the lily to Milly.
Milly took Billy Willy's lily
Down the hilly
And took a train to Philly.

--Jeanne Roller

A jolly old gentleman in our family could always get
the rapt attention of the children with his funny jingles and
strange sounding words. Our favorite of his sayings, long
remembered, was "Adda kwee pamjam, kumpown, fuqua da
bumbee." Where he got it or what it meant, we never knew
or asked; it was a fascinating entity in itself.

Eve Merriam well understands this gleeful attraction
for out-of-the-ordinary words in her books for children, particularly Rainbow Writing which is full of nonsense, laughter
and play with words. Another book with strong appeal to
the kind of humor enjoyed by children of all ages is Hurry,
Hurry Mary Dear by N. M. Bodecker, full of puns, refrains
and nonsense words. Both books are published by Atheneum
Publishers.

An interesting game to increase understanding of word
usage is the regional game. Explain that different localities
use a different word for the same thing. Begin with a common word, sofa and see how many children respond with
davenport or couch. Continue with other words having regional
usage:

pop--soda--soft drink
skillet--frying pan
counterpane--spread
faucet--spigot
park--green
brook--creek
sack--bag
turnpike--freeway
relatives--kinfolk

You may add words of your own to this list, and words that
the children may suggest. You may also continue with our
usage of words compared to English usage:

United States	England
gasoline	petrol
truck	lorry
streetcar	tram
wash cloth	wash rag
raincoat	mackintosh
cereal	porridge
crackers	biscuits
canned food	tinned food
faucet	tap
elevator	lift
subway	underground

A domino poem, sometimes called a crossword poem, is played by choosing a word--one with more than three letters is preferable--and writing it either vertically or horizontally. Then, beginning with one of the letters, write a new word, going in the opposite direction.

You might start with your own name:

```
S                          R A B B I T S

E                          T

L O S T                    E V E R Y

M    O                     E

A    M O N E Y             G R O W I N G

     E       E             E       N E I G H B O R S

             S             T             A

             T             A             R

             E             B             D

             R             L             E

             D             E             N

             A                           S

             Y
```

For interesting word play, try a "kenning," which is a compound word that may be familiar to students of English

literature courses. In Angle-Saxon and early Germanic
poetry, a kenning was used in place of a single noun, for
example, Swan-path (Sky) and Whale-road (Ocean). Have the
children make up some of their own, such as: Picture-box
(TV), Fire-box (Stove), or Star-garden (Sky). This play with
words might easily become another riddle game.

You may be inspired to invent warm-up games, spring-
boards, or pump-primers yourself as many teachers have
done. One of these which children found amusing and stimulating is called "Nashery." After reading poems by Ogden
Nash, older children enjoy making up words in the manner of
Mr. Nash, using imaginative, nonsensical rhyming words:
"Who wants my jellyfish? I'm not sellyfish." An example
of a "Nashery" is this inspired couplet:

> The practice of tomfoolery
> Is frowned upon in schoolery.

An interesting experiment is to try a conversation
poem by first reading a poem containing dialogue. An excellent one to begin with is "Overheard on a Saltmarsh" by
Harold Monro which is entirely in dialogue. The lively conversation between a nymph and a goblin is without quotation
marks, but it is easy to tell who is speaking. First is the
goblin, who demands the nymph's green glass beads, then
the nymph, who answers "No." Another favorite of children
is "Mummy Slept Late and Daddy Fixed Breakfast" by John
Ciardi, in which Daddy's remarks are enclosed in quotation
marks.

Asking the children to recall a strange or funny dream
often stimulates a rash of ideas. Some of the dreams present a nightmarish quality, some a wish fulfillment, some a
sensation such as flying or falling. All have an exciting
charm and unexpected imagery akin to a Dali painting or a
creation of the artist Chagall.

You might suggest writing a rhymed couplet by taking
a line from a well-known poem and making up a second line.
Usually the most absurd line is the most effective, such as
this one, frequently heard:

> The boy stood on the burning deck
> Eating peanuts by the peck.

This is, of course, more appealing than a logical second line
such as, "Flames shot up around his neck."

Another first-line springboard is to start with the line,
"The funniest thing I ever saw" or "The funniest thing I've
ever seen." My own contribution was shared with the group:

> The funniest thing I've ever seen
> Was a radish dancing with a bean.
> The radish was red and the bean was green.

The teacher or leader who is willing to participate in
activities and to share creative efforts with the children helps
them to become involved.

After you read a good poem orally to the children,
take time to enjoy colorful phrases and interesting words
with them. Bring in from your outside reading choice words,
phrases and descriptions--special words that are sweetly
musical, words that are thrilling to the tongue as we utter
them. It might be helpful to keep a notebook of these discoveries for children to browse through from time to time.
Soon they will be bringing in bits to read to you and the
group. They may even want to put together notebooks of
their own.

With all the possible activities to engage attention and
participation, a quiet time is important now and then for
listening to one's inner voice. Children need a time for med-
itation, a period of tranquility, a time to let their thoughts
wander and recall impressions that lie below the surface of
consciousness. William Wordsworth wrote in the preface to
Lyrical Ballads, "Poetry is the spontaneous overflow of
powerful feelings; it takes its origin from emotion recollected
in tranquility."

In order to allow the children to withdraw occasionally
from immediate surroundings, encourage gazing out the window,
not for the purpose of noting what can be seen in the way of a
tree, a stray dog, or a delivery turck but for allowing the
mind's eye to take over. A background of music is also
recommended, not for "listening to what the music says to
you," but for listening to what you are saying to yourself.
Images are filed away in memory, some near the surface
and some lie deeper. When a poet is writing, the inner eye
is free to capture images that bubble to the surface. Practicing poets have always understood the necessity and value of
daydreaming.

You will be able to enlarge your own store of tech-

niques and programs for helping children to discover their
creative inclinations and needs for poetry in the excellent
material available.   Books in hardback, books in paperback,
magazine articles, and articles in teachers' periodicals offer
practical suggestions, step-by-step guidelines, and stimulating
possibilities.

Not every procedure is suitable for every situation,
nor is every approach suitable for every individual, but with
plenty of material from which to pick and choose, you will
discover your own particular way to bring a lasting joy to
yourself and to the children.

How to Encourage Creative Poetry Writing

Almost every child can be inspired to write if first
stimulated by listening to poetry or by reading it.

Present poetry so that understanding and appreciation
can build as they grow.   Children need models just as other
artists do.   They need new dreams to dream over in solitude
and a time for laughter.

Mother Goose and nursery rhymes can be used for
language development, for dramatization, and for choral
speaking.

Truly appreciate poetry yourself and enjoy learning
with the children.   Through your involvement and enthusiasm,
they will discover the fun and satisfaction of poetry enter-
prises.   Write a poem of your own in class.

Include poems that explore contemporary life and
language, science, and politics.

Encourage using their own words, even slang, rather
than so-called "poetic" words.

A conversation period is an easy way to get started.
Share ideas before writing time.   Children enjoy telling about
something they have seen or experienced.   Listen to what
they say and what they are excited about.   Jot down notes
and read back later.   Often the beginning of a poem is found
there.

Encourage older children to write down their ideas as

quickly as they come on any scrap of paper or the back of
an envelope. Ideas sometimes have wings and fly away like
a butterfly. Later a poem fragment or idea can be transferred to a notebook for development and polishing.

Learn to recognize poetry which comes spontaneously
from a child. Children often speak in rhythmic language
under strong emotion.

Poetry is total involvement of mind and body. An
important attraction of poetry is found in rhythmic play im-
pulses, having fun with it and responding in a vigorous way.

Not all of the writing of children will be poetry, but
the games, the warm-up periods, play with words and experimenting with forms will add to self-confidence and provide
valuable practice for later development.

If anyone asks, "But is it poetry?" the answer is, "No,
not yet. But it is the stuff that poetry is made of."

A Guide to Evaluating Children's Writing

Look for virtues rather than defects. If one good
thing can be pointed out, the child has a feeling of achievement and can build on that one good thing. Compliment a
good line or a good word; praise in whole or in part. Encourage reading their poems aloud, but never insist.

Look for the following:

Singing quality through rhythm, cadence, repetition
    or refrain.
Words rich in sensory appeal.
Imagery--pictures painted with words.
Feelings that reflect the child's true reactions.
Meanings that give value to impressions.
Originality in thought, feelings, or expression.
Interesting form, pattern, or stucture.
Subjects that may be expressed with words of rhythm
    and magic imagery.
Unforced rhymes and unusual rhymes.
Fun. Poetry is not always serious and solemn. It
    can laugh, chuckle, and make jokes.

Avoid criticism that makes a child afraid of making

mistakes or of not pleasing. Spelling, punctuation, neatness, and form are not the prime goals and often stop the flow of ideas. Polishing a poem should come after it is created.

The best poetry written by children is that which springs from true feelings.

SUGGESTIONS FOR FURTHER READING

Teaching and Appreciating Poetry with Children

Adoff, Arnold. It Is the Poem Singing into Your Eyes. New York: Harper & Row, 1971.

Alexander, Arthur. The Poet's Eye. New Jersey: Prentice-Hall, 1967.

Anderson, Douglas. My Sister Looks Like a Pear. New York: Hart Publishing Co. , 1974.

Applegate, Mauree. Helping Children Write. Evanston, IL: Row-Peterson, 1954.

Arnstein, Flora J. Children Write Poetry. New York: Dover Publications, 1967.

Arnstein, Flora J. Poetry in the Elementary Classroom. New York: Appleton-Century-Crofts, 1962.

Baldwin, Michael. Poetry Without Tears. Boston: Routledge, 1959.

Behn, Harry. Chrysalis (Concerning Children & Poetry). New York: Harcourt-Brace, 1949.

Bolton, Eric J. Verse Writing in Schools. Elmsford, N. Y. : Pergamon, 1966.

Chukovsky, Karnei. From Two to Five. Translated and edited by Miriam Morton. California: University of California Press, 1971.

Ciardi, John. You Read to Me, I'll Read to You. New York:
    Lippincott, 1962.

Hopkins, Lee Bennett. Pass the Poetry, Please. New York:
    Citation Press, 1972.

Hughes, Rosalind. Let's Enjoy Poetry. Boston: Houghton-
    Mifflin, 1958.

Hughes, Ted. Poetry Is. New York: Doubleday, 1970.

Johnson, Sickels, Sayers, and Horovitz. Anthology of Chil-
    dren's Literature. 5th Edition. Boston: Houghton-
    Mifflin. Co. , 1977.

Joseph, Stephen M. The Me Nobody Knows: Children's
    Voices from the Ghetto. New York: World Publishing,
    1969.

Kimsey, Ardis. To Defend a Form. New York: Teachers
    & Writers, 1977.

Koch, Kenneth. Rose, Where Did You Get That Red? New
    York: Vintage Books, div. of Random House,
    1974.

Koch, Kenneth. Wishes, Lies & Dreams. New York: Chel-
    sea House, 1970.

Larrick, Nancy. Green Is Like a Meadow of Grass. Illinois:
    Garrard, 1968.

Larrick, Nancy. I Heard a Scream in the Street. Philadel-
    phia: Lippincott, 1970.

Larrick, Nancy. Somebody Turned on a Tap in These Kids.
    (Poetry & Young People Today), New York: Dela-
    corte, 1971.

Lewis, Richard. Miracles, Poems by Children of the English-
    Speaking World. New York: Simon & Schuster, 1969.

Lewis, Richard. The Wind & The Rain (Children's Poems).
    New York: Simon & Schuster, 1968.

Livingston, Myra Cohn. When You Are Alone/It Keeps You
    Capone. New York: Atheneum, 1973.

Lopate, Phillip. Being with Children. New York: Doubleday,
     1975.

Merriam, Eve. There Is No Rhyme for Silver. New York:
     Atheneum, 1962.

Merriam, Eve. It Doesn't Always Have to Rhyme. New York:
     Atheneum, 1964.

Merriam, Eve. Catch a Little Rhyme. New York: Atheneum,
     1966.

Merriam, Eve. Finding a Poem. New York: Atheneum,
     1970.

Merriam, Eve. Out Loud. New York: Atheneum, 1970.

Merriam, Eve. Rainbow Writing. New York: Atheneum,
     1976.

Painter, Helen W. Poetry and Children. Delaware: Interna-
     tional Reading Association, 1970.

Petty, Walter T. , and Bowen, Mary E. Slithery Snakes and
     Other Aids to Children's Writing. New York: Apple-
     ton-Century-Crofts, 1967.

Swenson, May. Poems To Solve. New York: Charles
     Scribner, 1966.

Swenson, May. More Poems to Solve. New York: Charles
     Scribner.

Walsh, Chad. Doors to Poetry. New Jersey: Prentice-Hall,
     1970.

Wiener, Harvey S. Any Child Can Write. New York: Mc-
     Graw-Hill, 1978.

Wolsch, Robert A. Poetic Composition Through the Grades.
     New York: Teachers College Press, 1970.

INDEX